From Diversity to Unity

From Diversity to Unity

Southern and Appalachian Migrants in Uptown Chicago, 1950–1970

ROGER GUY

LEXINGTON BOOKS

A division of
ROWMAN & LITTLEFIELD PUBLISHERS, INC.
Lanham • Boulder • New York • Toronto • Plymouth, UK

Published by Lexington Books
A division of Rowman & Littlefield Publishers, Inc.
A wholly owned subsidiary of The Rowman & Littlefield Publishing Group, Inc.
4501 Forbes Boulevard, Suite 200, Lanham, Maryland 20706
http://www.lexingtonbooks.com

Estover Road, Plymouth PL6 7PY, United Kingdom

British Library Cataloguing in Publication Information Available

Library of Congress Cataloging-in-Publication Data
Guy, Roger, 1960–
 From diversity to unity : Southern and Appalachian migrants in Uptown Chicago, 1950–1970 / Roger Guy.
    p. cm.
 Includes bibliographical references.
 1. City and town life—Illinois—Chicago—History. 2. Neighborhood—Illinois—Chicago—History. 3. Rural-urban migration—Southern States—History. 4. Appalachians (People)—Migrations. I. Title.
 HT384.U52C45 2007
 307.7609773'11—dc22   2007038125

ISBN: 978-0-7391-1833-7 (cloth : alk. paper)
ISBN: 978-0-7391-1834-4 (pbk. : alk. paper)
ISBN: 978-0-7391-4087-1 (electronic)

Printed in the United States of America

Contents

Maps and Figures

Acknowledgements

In what seems like long ago, I was in a seminar on qualitative research in which the ethnographer, Elijah Anderson was present. Here was the sage talking to a group of young eager graduate students at the University of Wisconsin-Milwaukee. When it came time for questions, I asked Anderson what I should choose as a topic for research. He paused and said, "Do who you are." I did not know what he meant immediately, but I knew that I was southern white migrant in the Midwest. After some reflection and direction from my advisor John Zipp, I located my first contact in Uptown who had worked with southern white migrants. I am indebted to these two men for inspiring me to undertake this work. After beginning research my advisor, Joseph A. Rodriguez provided enormous support to complete it as a dissertation. His confidence and optimism made the original draft of this work possible.

In Uptown, the initial interviews were possible because southerners spoke on my behalf. The first time that Belinda Belcher took me to meet her father, Bill he was so throughly unimpressed with my desire to conduct research that he politely shut the door on us. Eventually he and his wife Clara let me into their home, and I spent countless afternoons spent with them in their apartment in Uptown. Most of the time my visits had nothing to do with my research. I refused to consider them part of research. I consider them as my family. Their daughter Belinda provided me with numerous subjects to interview, and allowed frequent access to her kitchen, back porch, and Bud Light. In the process of conducting research I learned that their warmth and generosity were unlimited. There were many other southern migrants that helped me along the way. Virginia Bowers and Sarah Dotson allowed me to glimpse the human struggle and cost of migration. Violent McKnight taught me the value of listening to subjects.

Librarians and archivists were instrumental in providing the documents and suggestions for my work. Shannon Wilson, Gerald Roberts, and Sidney Farr at the Hutchins Library at Barea College spent hours locating materials and offering words of encouragement. The librarians at the Municipal Reference Collection, and the Harold Washington Library, and Chicago Historical Society helped immensely during the early stages of my work. The Sultzer Regional Library in Chicago provided unlimited access to the microfilmed, *Edgewater-Uptown News* and *Uptown News*.

Others have given me professional and emotional support over the years. Phil Obermiller gave me professional opportunities to present and publish my research. He has been a friend and mentor helping me to navigate my way through the conference and publication processes. Raleigh Campbell read drafts of the chapter on the Chicago Southern Center of which he was a director. His comments were invaluable. Lewis Killian, the original author of work on white southerners in Chicago gave me his approval to proceed with my research. Chad Berry, my partner in crime, opened his house for me and listened to my ideas. His support and professional accomplishments made me continue my work.

My wife, Yoshiko, meticulously read drafts of all the chapters. She is a gifted graphic designer. She completed all the visual material contained in these pages. She also believed in me, and remained by my side in spite of my shortcomings. Any comfort or joy that I experience in life is in some way connected to her. Chris Galvan and John McCullagh proofread early drafts of the manuscript. Their young eyes and keen suggestions improved the flow and clarity of the final draft.

This book is really my small attempt to honor and capture the experience of the southern families who made the journey to Chicago. Since being interviewed many have passed away. This work is a dedicated to them.

Introduction

Prelude to Departure

There are certain street corners in this town that have a city wide reputation. These reputations continue even though the basis for that rep' is gone. I was born in Chicago. When I was coming up in the forties, if you said Halsted and Taylor that meant the Sons of Italy, an Italian gang. In Uptown, Wilson and Broadway was known for the southern whites in the fifties and sixties.[1]

It was Friday morning when Donald Powell got to Chicago. It was 1963 and he was almost seventeen. The rain was battering the windshield so hard that it was difficult to see. He had left Tuscaloosa, Alabama behind two days before. As so many other southerners his would be a cycle of leaving and returning to the South. Returning to Tuscaloosa would not always be under auspicious circumstances. He had been to Chicago once before when he had run away from home to live with his mother in Cicero. When his step father refused to let him stay, his mother left and took Donald back to Tuscaloosa in what would result in a deadly trip for one of his friends. This time he felt like he was one of the last to leave Tuscaloosa or the South for that matter. Donald's brother lived in an apartment in Uptown. Most of his friends had left Tuscaloosa for places in the Midwest like so many other southerners during the same time period. Donald had even heard a rumor that the former governor of West Virginia was driving a cab in Chicago. Donald's grandfather, a jailer, and his grandmother remained in Tuscaloosa. He has been raised by the couple from an early age. He parked the car in the alley behind his brother's apartment building on Clifton Street in Uptown. He was unprepared for the blast of cold rain when he got out of the car. Beyond the noise and strangeness of the city, he felt immersed in familiarity. There were license plates from Kentucky, West Virginia, and Alabama. People looked down at him from back porches and fire escapes. The building was crowded with faces he imagined that he recognized. Even the yelling coming from an open window made him feel at ease. He knew what their looks meant, and felt at home in a city that would not always welcome someone from the South. On Monday Donald went to Bell and Howell in Skokie with a friend, Billy Peña. Billy worked on the production line making Swinger cameras. He told Donald to lie about his age on the application. Later that day Donald was sitting on the front stoop of the building with a job. Eventually he was promoted to supervisor. It would not be long until Donald would leave Chicago again with his girlfriend, Brenda, who was expecting his daughter. Soon he was back in Uptown single again. Twenty six years later when I interviewed him, he had still not seen his daughter. Donald's life reflected one segment of southern white who migrated to Chicago between 1950 and 1970. He drank too much. He had not held stable work for some years. The promise of mobility in an America rapidly losing well-paying jobs had not materialized. Yet he remained committed to Uptown as a place, as an idea for southerners. Although he lived north of Uptown in an area known as Rogers Park. He referred to himself as an "Uptown boy." Like so many other southern whites, he found Uptown less affordable that it once was. However he had been in Chicago most of his adult life. The Uptown that he spoke existed in the past, when he had more money when that he won playing pool at the Golden Goose tavern. Perhaps Powell was among the unlucky, I thought. Perhaps those southern migrants who had achieved stability and mobility had left for the suburbs or gone back home.

For at least twenty years the Chicago community area known as Uptown and southern whites were synonymous. Older clusters of white Southerners have been studied in the North Center Community in Chicago as early as 1920, but the area never received such notorious reputation as did Uptown. Killian authored the original study of southern white laborers on the near west side of Chicago.[2] As a southerner himself, Killian was able to easily make contact with his lower class brethren in Chicago. Like many researchers influenced by Robert Park, Killian studied them by examining their relationship to their port of entry community. As the quote at the beginning of the introduction suggests, Uptown is remembered as a port of entry for southern whites where outsiders were not always welcome. Southern whites took pride in calling Uptown "Hillbilly Heaven" as so many did. Southern youth fought youth from other ethnic groups for control of streets. Southern migrants initially settled in pockets of Uptown, sometimes according to the county of origin. For example, clusters of migrants from specific counties lived on a street dubbed "Tennessee Street" by the migrants and their neighbors.

As the influx of southern whites increased, so did their attention from the media. Beginning in the 1950s, newspapers began to link southerners and Uptown. "Hillbilly Heaven" invoked a sense of pride among some southerners, and fear and disdain to Chicagoans. To the cops Uptown was another problem to handle, another domestic dispute, another drunk, another knife fight. At the height of this migration, between 1950 and 1970, little was written about Uptown in the press without some mention of southern whites, or hillbillies. Today, most Chicagoans recall the notorious reputation southerners gave the corner of Wilson and Broadway at the height of the southern migration. While the source of the reputation has waned with the recent forced evacuation of southerners, and rapid gentrification in Uptown, the reputation endures in the minds of many Chicagoans. Moreover, movies like *Next of Kin* have rekindled this reputation in a nostalgic way. Patrick Swayze as the proud hillbilly Chicago cop, and Liam Neeson as the brother from down home seeking revenge in Uptown added a new dimension to the idea of hillbillies in Uptown. As so many movies it legitimized stereotypical behavior associated with

Appalachian whites. Snake handling, moonshine, violence, and a lack of hygiene all become part of the backdrop which authenticated southern whites in Uptown. The movie pits the hillbillies against the mob in another version of David and Goliath.

There were certain features of cities that affected all migrants. The terms of racial contact were different. Southern whites underwent important personal changes when they interacted with African Americans and Latinos in ways that were new. In the South, racial norms and etiquette shaped interaction between whites and non-whites. In the North these racial lines were blurred and contact was often not as clearly defined as in the Jim Crow South. Compared to many parts of the South, Chicago was more densely populated, required more familiarity with public transportation, and was more racially heterogeneous.

Of the thousands of southern whites that migrated to industrial centers of the Midwest between 1950 and 1970, Chicago was a unique destination for several reasons. The first was geographic proximity. In Cincinnati a person only needed to cross the Ohio River into Cincinnati to be classified as a migrant from Kentucky. Migration to Chicago was more selective, and more heterogeneous than regional destinations within the South, or contiguous states. One could even argue that culturally Cincinnati was more like the South than Chicago.

Migrants came from more diverse places geographically, and differed in their reasons for coming, and habits of mobility. Some migrants would return to home frequently while others rarely returned unless compelled to do so. It should not be assumed that merely because migrants were all from the South, they shared any pre-existing solidarity. One observer commented at the time that, "a coal miner from West Virginia and a farmer from Alabama have little in common. Only persons in the city assume they do."[3] This is an important point because it reveals how southern migrants were perceived by others.

Uptown was important in understanding particularity of the southern white experience in Chicago because it was undergoing rapid change from being a desirable residential and commercial location in the early part of the Twentieth Century to an area of seedy bars and decaying multi-family apartments that had been cheaply converted in the Postwar era. Up until World War II, Uptown boasted some of the finest hotels and night life in Chicago. The success of the area as an entertainment district rather than a residential area carried the seeds of decline. Beginning in the 1940s, a housing shortage led to the conversion of older hotels into rooming houses. The demand for housing during the war and the arrival of white Southern migrants in the 1950s and 1960s led landlords to divide many of the spacious apartments into smaller single occupancy dwellings. Moreover, because rapid decline coincided with their arrival in Uptown, southern whites were linked with neighborhood blight.

Chicago's Uptown community area was also unique to the southern whites migrant experience because of the intense community activism that occurred due in part to groups like the Students for a Democratic Society and the Black Panthers. During the 1960s southern whites participated in campaigns to eradicate poor housing conditions and police brutality. Community organizations in the 1970s faced an aggressive campaign of forced evictions, intimidation and arson. According to some, this was an attempt by developers to rid the community of its poor residents and free up property for more lucrative development. Numerous southern whites had died in arson-related fires during the 1980s.[4] The construction of Harry S. Truman College and Pensacola Place (a high rise housing development and supermarket) in the seventies was the final blow to the southern whites. The bulk of their population was displaced by these two projects. Today, only a few of the original migrant families remain in Uptown.

Finally Chicago became a Mecca for southern white migrants. Although other cities received more southern migrants, they never referred to any other destination as "Hillbilly Heaven". As mentioned above, this area was mythologized in song, legend, and later in a commercial film, titled *Next of Kin* in which migrants had acting roles, or served as consultants. To most Chicagoans at the time, Uptown was a "hillbilly ghetto." As with many other racial and ethnic groups the depiction of disadvantaged groups often varies with the times. Up until the novel and film adaptation of Pearl S. Buck's, *The Good Earth* most Chinese in America were associated with a "yellow peril" that brought on violence, hostility and eventual exclusion from immigrating to the United States with the passage of the Chinese Exclusion Act in 1882. Before the thousands of southerners migrated to Chicago, most Chicagoans who had never seen southerners derived their perceptions from the novel *The Grapes of Wrath*, or the television show *The Beverly Hillbillies*. This gave an entirely different impression to Chicagoans than what they observed with Appalachian and southern migrants. Instead of the humble, rural, agricultural laborer in search of the American dream, or the happy go lucky hillbilly, most migrants lived in crowded, dilapidated apartments, and appeared to many to not be looking for work, but the next drink or knife fight. They were menacing and unfamiliar. They were dirty and uncouth. In an era in America characterized by expanding suburbs and affluence seemingly available to all who desired it, the southern migrant became a reminder of the limits social class placed on achieving the American dream. Most ignored the structural impediments such as the inability of the economy to absorb all the migrants. Instead, migrants were criticized on the basis of deficient cultural, moral, and social characteristics. Poverty was seen as proof of southern sloth and degeneracy. Most people wanted to forget southern whites in cities.

Not surprisingly, exaggerated accounts in the Chicago media of southern migrants began appearing in the 1950s. Unlike the humble Okie, The drunken urban mountaineer walking the streets of Chicago was a menacing figure that struck fear in the minds of readers. This stereotype would remain as southerners continued to arrive in Chicago throughout the twentieth century. For those in Uptown who had never encountered southern whites or Appalachians, the series of articles written by Norma Browning were the only source of information for some Chicagoans. The article, "Girl Reporter Visits Hillbilly Jungle" written in 1957 typified this form of media sensationalism. In the article, Browning portrays southern whites as the worst group to arrive in Chicago:

> Skid row dives, opium parlors and assorted other dens of inequity collectively are safe as Sunday school picnics compared with the joints taken over by clans of fightin' and feudin' southern hillbillies and their shootin' cousins, who today constitute one of the most dangerous and lawless elements of Chicago's fastest growing migrant population.[5]

This image shaped the perception of southern migrants in Chicago and created an unwelcome environment for them. Like so many ethnic groups before them, southern migrants faced occupational and housing discrimination. In a rare instance one southern white even appealed to the National Association for the Advancement of Colored People (NAACP) after being refused service at a Chicago restaurant.[6] Most surviving documents paint a fairly monolithic picture of southern white migrants as a social problem. Few observers understood how the forces of change in the community affected the plight of the migrants or how the migrants themselves viewed their community. The negative association of the corner of Wilson and Broadway eclipsed the lives of those southerners who struggled to work and raise their families any way they could in a neighborhood constantly threatened by external forces such as unemployment, urban redevelopment, gentrification and a deindustrializing economic base. Those few academic accounts of southern migrants failed to consider the way in which southerners were forging community in the process of struggling to survive.

Urban adjustment and community building among migrant groups is a prominent theme for historians and sociologists. Some have argued that nascent urban migrant communities served as "decompression chambers" for the migrant generation as they assimilated into the dominant American culture. Others have viewed international migrants as culturally fragmented groups adapting to the demands of a capitalist economy.[7] Writers in this vein have argued that nationality was the basis of ethnic identity and community. Class and culture are seen as primary mechanisms of social organization. The topic of southern migration to northern and mid-western cities has received wide attention. Although, the preponderance of this work has centered on the African American experience there are exceptions.[8] Historical work on the southern white experience in mid-western cities has not received as much attention as the African-American experience for numerous reasons, among them the invisibility of southern whites in official records.[9] Still there is some sociological work on southern white urban migration.[10] Historical work on white migrants has addressed several issues relevant to southern white identity and community. In an earlier work, James Gregory discussed the emergence of an Okie subculture in California. More recently Chad Berry and James Gregory have refuted previous stereotypes regarding the lack of mobility among southern migrants in the North.[11] Similar to immigrants, this work assumes that migrants bring an identifiable culture with them before arrival that is malleable, which aids in survival and group consciousness. In this work I take the position that most southerners had no inherent identity in the ethnic sense before coming to Chicago. Individuals make up mass movements of people, and as such individual needs and familial bonds occupy a prominent position in their minds before a sense of identity as a group. Once in Uptown similarities of kin, county, and finally region evolved into an identity and solidarity.

The idea here is that the presence of a critical mass of southerners, the development of key institutions, and the neighborhood's vital street life played key roles in the emergence of a unique southern identity among these urban migrants. It was in the context of this environment that southerners forged a reluctant but thriving identity and community. As many foreign immigrants southern migrants brought no inherent identity in the ethnic sense to Chicago. In the South regional appellations and even identity based on one's county took precedence over being southern.[12] Just as some European migrants, southern migrants came from diverse regions, had varying class origins, and personal experiences.[13] However it was only at their destination in the North that any larger group consciousness emerged. The identity and community that emerged in Uptown was, in part, a response to the hostile reception that migrants received, and their ability to draw upon a common notion of the South and the migration experience.

Once in Chicago geographic concentration helped forge unity among southern migrants. This unity was furthered by similar experiences in Chicago which separated them from those who remained in the South. Part of this had to do with the historic evolution of Uptown as a self-sufficient community. Southerners did not have to rely on the Loop for shopping nor leave their community except to go to work. In addition, stereotypes, discrimination and harsh treatment solidified this migrant identity and further entrenched the community. This made southerners hard to reach socially and official agencies had difficulty solving migrant social problems.

Over time, the most successful organized efforts to aid migrants worked because they appealed to migrants as southerners. Originally the Chicago Southern Center emphasized pride in being southern, and the Students for a Democratic Society's JOIN (Jobs of Income Now) program channeled this nascent southern identity and cohesion in the direction of social activism which survives today. This was bolstered by successful protests against poor housing and police brutality. As southerners fought for their neighborhood, they strengthened their identity, unity and attachment to Uptown. As such, southerners had a central role in shaping the destiny of the community of Uptown. Perhaps this was best realized with the planned construction of Hank Williams Village in Uptown. This multi-use housing and retail development was to be named after the legendary country singer. They were not passive victims, but active participants in their community. The unity and common experience in Chicago fostered a sense of a common identity among southern migrants. A common concept of home, developed after migrating to Chicago, unified migrants in the face of stereotypes and hostile treatment.

Chapter one discusses the personal experiences of people leaving home and coming to Chicago, and the push and pull factors influencing the mass exodus of people from different parts of the South. My point is to demonstrate in a loose way that migrants were not a monolithic group. Many may assume that all were displaced miners, for example. I am not attempting to draw analytic distinctions or explain how these seemingly diverse origins influenced behavior and thinking on the part of migrants. I am merely trying to engage the assumption that all migrants were hillbillies from Appalachia as most press accounts assumed. The voices of the migrants reveal the personal struggle most experienced after arriving, and capture the disappointment and exhilaration that people lived though. Uncovering their lives shows that migration is a human endeavor that people experienced as individuals. I am not implying that larger social and economic changes should not be used or minimized in understanding migration. These forces should serve as a backdrop for the southern diaspora that ensued. In addition, I want to show the significant role that women played in the migration process. Concentrating solely on the larger push and pull factors tends to inadvertently relegate women to the background of the historical narrative. The women interviewed for this work took an active role in the timing and decision to leave home. Often overlooked are the single women who left their families in the South, attracted by the glamor and excitement of the city.

Chapter two shows that the social, economic and geographic evolution of Uptown facilitated southern migrant unity. Uptown evolved separately from the Loop, the retail and commercial center of Chicago, as a center for retail, commerce and entertainment center. The physical and geographic boundaries of Uptown helped isolate southern migrants from other neighborhoods. At the height of migration, the low cost housing attracted migrants to Uptown. Although much of this housing was dilapidated from years of neglect, it was affordable to migrants. Eventually the efforts of conservation groups reduced some of the overcrowded and substandard housing, however, the age of the housing stock, and the steady influx of migrants exacerbated problems in the area and put them on a collision course with older residents in Uptown. As most urban newcomers southern whites chose the most affordable housing possible. Much of the housing was dilapidated from years of neglect and conversions to smaller units. Eventually southern whites became associated with the cause of neighborhood decline. Like so many others before them southerners were but another scapegoat for the neighborhood conditions.[14]

Today Uptown remains a port of entry. Following the arrival of southern whites in the 1960s, Native Americans came to Uptown along with Puerto Ricans. In the 1970s Latinos and African Americans moved in attracted by the cheap and public housing. In the 1980s and 1990s sill more newcomers arrived. Africans, refugees from Southeast Asia and the former Soviet Union settled along with hundreds of de-institutionalized mentally ill. More recently urban professionals escaping higher priced property in other neighborhoods have begun to take advantage of a growing sector of condominiums. Following these more affluent newcomers have been athletic clubs and Borders. These businesses coexist with remnants of the past like Carols Pub on Clark Street, a country western bar frequented by southern whites who remain in Uptown, and Shake Rattle and Read, a used bookstore. Uptown is a postmodern human menagerie. If you stand at the corner of Broadway and Lawrence you are as likely to bump into an immigrant from Ghana or Mexico as you are a punk heading to a show in the Rivera Theater. All three may have stopped at Pho 777 for a bowl of Vietnamese noodles. I can't help but to think that some of the older residents from the South view all this with a tinge of melancholy. Times have changed, people are as unfamiliar as when they arrived from Kentuck or West Virginia. Now, however, it is harder to adapt to newer surroundings and different people. There are far fewer southern whites in Uptown as there were in the 1960s. It is unclear where they went. Some were displaced by gentrification, while others were able to move out to the suburbs or back to the South.

Chapter three addresses how a sense of unity developed among southern migrants based on their common experiences adapting to the urban environment and the uniqueness of Chicago. Southern migrants had to adjust to racial norms that were different from their places of origin in the South. Although Chicago was heavily segregated, there were more occasions for races to interact than in the South. In addition this interaction was on more equal footing than in the South. There was more danger in the city. There were more strangers. There were unfamiliar places. This was unsettling. The process of migration and urban adjustment eventually differentiated those who remained in the South from those who left. Similar to immigrants who find themselves separated from their homes and kinfolk, southern migrants developed a sort of exile mentality which influenced how migrants understood the South and Chicago. Part of this involved romanticizing the places they left in the South. The South as a homeland evolved as a kind of mythic place and became inherent in their identity as migrants in the North. Because they were also separated from their friends and kin that they had left behind, this migrant identity evolved from similar sets of experiences in Chicago. This set them apart from their southern brethren. In short what it meant to be southern in the South became very different than what it meant to be southern in the North.

Chapter four argues that negative stereotypes from the media, police and the long-time residents of Uptown encouraged a sense of unity among southern whites. It forced them to defend themselves against the assumption that they were the cause of neighborhood decline and crime. In addition, this assault from without facilitated a sense of common southern identity. While the media portrayed their neighborhoods as crime-ridden and filthy, southern migrants had the opposite impression of their neighborhood reflecting a newly-found pride and unity. The unwanted stereotype of the southern white migrant as a petty criminal or irresponsible drunkard remained. Southerners had little ability to resist the label without effective advocacy or an organization working on their behalf.

Chapter five traces the origin and development of the Chicago Southern Center. The CSC was the first organization to connect with southern migrants. Most southern whites avoided any contact with social welfare organizations. As an extension of the Council of the Southern Mountains based in Berea, Kentucky, the CSC sought to emphasize urban assimilation and adaptation. Their programs centered around southern culture and practical services. Job placement and emergency food as well as cultural activities like quilting were all offered at the Chicago Southern Center. Because it was centered around the notion of being southern, the CSC strengthened southern identity and unity. Moreover, the clout of some members affiliated with the CSC, such as W. Clement Stone resulted in more positive media coverage southern migrants. This ameliorated the public perception of southern white migrants in Uptown.

Chapter six shows that a movement initiated by the Students for a Democratic Society called, Jobs or Income Now (JOIN) added a different dimension to what it meant to be southern in Uptown. To be southern meant to fight police brutality and poor housing. While the Chicago Southern Center had a distinctive assimilation focus characteristic of the 1950s, Jobs or Income Now was an outgrowth of the movement for civil rights and social equality. These two groups were significantly different in their aims and tactics. The members of JOIN were more effective at identifying and mobilizing a disadvantaged segment of the southern whites in Uptown. Rent strikes, picketing buildings, and direct forms of social protest were all used by JOIN. The transition of southern migrants to social activists and limited success of social protest reinforced their attachment to Uptown and bolstered their common southern identity. Southerners eventually took ownership of their community by assuming leadership roles in social protest. The most obvious expression of this was a near successful construction of Hank Williams Village in Uptown.

Chapter seven argues that in spite of the successes in social protest and community activism, thousands of southern migrants were displaced by force through arson and the construction of Harry S. Truman College and Pensacola Place. This wiped out blocks with the largest concentrations of southern migrants. Southern migrants today are largely invisible among the newest groups of immigrants struggling to survive in Uptown. However, strands of social protest remain in Uptown and are changing to meet the needs of newer groups of multi-cultural immigrants arriving from Asia and the Americas.

Notes

1. Personal interview by the author with Edward Kennedy, Department of Human Services, City of Chicago, 2 February 1994.
2. Lewis Killian, "Southern White Laborers in Chicago's West Side" (Unpublished Ph.D. diss., University of Chicago, 1949).
3. Harry Woodward, "The Southern White Migrant in Lakeview" (Unpublished report for the Lakeview Citizens Council, 1962), 26.
4. "Murder by Fire," *Keep Strong,* February, 1980:5–12; Personal interview by the author with Walter "Slim" Coleman, 8 October 1992.
5. Norma Lee Browning, "Girl Reporter Visits Jungles of Hillbillies," *Chicago Daily Tribune*, 7 March 1957, 1(N).
6. Untitled, *Chicago Daily Defender,* 23 March 1957.

7. Oscar Handlin, *The Uprooted: The Epic Story of the Great Migrations that Made the American People* (Boston: Little Brown, 1951); John Bodner, *The Transplanted* (Bloomington: Indiana University Press, 1987); David Ward, *Poverty, Ethnicity and the American City, 1840–1925* (Cambridge: Cambridge University Press, 1989).

8. On the African American experience see for example James Grossman, *Land of Hope: Chicago, Black Southerners and the Great Migration* (Chicago: University of Chicago Press, 1989).

9. Unlike migrant groups that can be tracked by race or surname, southern whites remain nearly "invisible" in census and other traditional primary sources. As a result, oral histories, local newspapers, and municipal reports make up the bulk of the primary sources in the book. Because Uptown's population was over 98 percent caucasian, place of origin data from the census was particularly useful to support the oral histories.

10. Killian, "Southern White Laborers in Chicago's West Side," and Edwin S. Harwood, "Work and Community Among Southern Migrants to Chicago" (Unpublished Ph.D. diss., University of Chicago, 19660, Todd Gitlin and Nanci Hollander, *Uptown: Poor Whites in Chicago* (New York: Harper and Row, 1970).

11. James Gregory, *American Exodus: The Dust Bowl Migration and Okie Culture in California* (New York: Oxford University Press, 1989), Chad Berry, *Southern Migrants: Northern Exiles* (Chicago: University of Illinois Press, 2000), James Gregory, *The Southern Diaspora: How the Great Migrations of Black and White Southerners Transformed America* (Chapel Hill: University of North Carolina Press, 2005).

12. Robert M. Ireland, *Little Kingdoms: The Counties of Kentucky* (Lexington: University Press of Kentucky, 1977).

13. Jacqueline Jones, *The Dispossessed: America's Underclasses from the Civil War to the Present* (New York: Basic Books, 1992).

14. Historical examples are numerous involving immigrant groups in cities such as, Irish and Italian immigrants in the Five Points section of New York City and San Francisco's Chinatown. Contemporary immigrants from Asia and Latin America and minorities in deteriorating inner cities are often associated with the cause of urban decay and social problems.

Chapter 1

Hitting the Hillbilly Highway:
Leaving Home Behind

When I left Man [West Virginia] I was a waitress. I had a girl friend who was going to visit her brother here in Uptown and I went with her. Most of my friends from high school had left Man for places like New York or other cities and I wanted to go see Chicago. I'd never traveled in my life. I'd never left the area. But I had it in my mind that if I liked it there I would stay. I told my boss if I liked it in Chicago I would let him know to replace me.[1]

Sarah Dotson grew up in Williamson, West Virginia in the 1940s. Daily life was difficult, but the close family, community, and the beauty of West Virginia made up for the lack of material comfort. The only heat for the house was a wood stove, and the clapboard siding left ample room for drafts during the winter, and insects during the summer. It was only after she had left Williamson that Sarah realized how little that this had bothered her. The quiet evenings and proximity of nature somehow made up for the lack of urban amenities. Sarah and her husband, Thurman left for Chicago in 1957. As she saw it, there was not much of a choice if the family was going to survive. Thurman was working sporadically. Unemployment was running as high as 30 percent. Strip mining, absentee mineral owners, and decades of mechanization had robbed the land and people of much hope of staying where they were born and raised. She left behind her life and all that came with it. She left the blue glass Mason jar of her favorite pebbles that she collected from the creek. She left the graves of her kinfolk that passed away before her, and the opportunity to be buried beside them. She left all that composed life and identity back home. She didn't know then that she would become one of the founders of the Chicago Area Black Lung Association.

The only other time Sarah had left Williamson was to travel to the hospital to give birth to her children. She was afraid to leave West Virginia, but she believed that it was the only way to provide for her family. The fear she experienced was mixed with a determination to succeed, and a certain naivete that produced a willingness to go to Chicago. She could always return, she thought. Word had spread back to Williamson, that there was plenty of work, and she knew other family members that lived in Uptown. During World War II, other kinfolk had been to Chicago and Detroit and had returned home with their own tales of urban life and the abundant work available. Sarah described to me how she left Williamson:

> My husband's work played out on him in the mines, no saw mills, couldn't cut no timber so he left and went to Chicago. He was supposed to go get a job. He had six or seven cousins up here over on Racine [a popular street for southern white settlement in Uptown]. So where he worked they owed him some money. So I decided that I know what he's gonna do. He's gonna go up there, cause they were begging him to come but he didn't want to, and gonna go up there and he's gonna come back and tell me that he couldn't find a job. So I figured I'd go pick his check up [his boss passed by the foot of the mountain every morning at 6:30] So one morning I got up about six o'clock, got dressed and I met him at the foot of the mountain, and I got my husband's check. I brought it to the grocery store. I got 'em to cash it. So I said to them, now at eleven o'clock I want you to come and pick me and the kids up cause we are going to Chicago. They said, 'what! I can't believe it!' I said Thurman's gone up there and he's gonna tell people that he can't find a job so he can hit it back to the house. And I'm gonna be up there. I wanted to be there so I could go to work. So when I got on the bus here he'd done got on a bus up there going the other way. So when he got here I was gone and when I got there he was gone[2]

Sarah's story of departure is as unique as it is characteristic of many who left Appalachia in the Postwar era for cities in the Midwest. It is similar to many stories of migrants because it points out the traditional economic factors and the role of kin in migration and settlement. More often than not when we think of interregional or international migration the economic factors come to mind as well as the important part families play in helping out those who leave home. Often it is a family member at the place of destination that urges people to migrate thereby completing the bridge from place to place. In this case Thurman's cousins wanted him to come to Uptown to get a job in Chicago. According to Sarah, Thurman expressed no interest in leaving home. It was Sarah that worked out a way to ensure that he would remain in Uptown by taking the initiative to join him. Another uncharacteristic aspect about Sarah's story involves gender. Most work written on the postwar migration of millions of white Appalachians or southerners has focused on the male experience.[3] By and large the voice of women remains conspicuously absent or subsumed within the family in works on migration. Women are seen as playing a support role at best in this historic movement of people.[4] Recently it has been argued that this is due in part to the "frameworks of theory and empirical investigation" that have dominated research[5] Sarah's narrative reveals the important role women played in migration. There was considerable risk involved in leaving Williamson with the little money that the family had. Sarah's willingness to "go for broke" is indicative of the strong desire to leave West Virginia, and hope she had for her family in Chicago. It was not desperation but rather, inspiration on her part. She was inspired by the tales others had brought back from Chicago, the knowledge that others would be waiting for her in Chicago, and the desire to lift her family out of poverty. Throughout this section of the interview, Sarah emphasized her desire to find a job and work. She was eager to locate employment. Thurman's reluctance to go to Chicago and Sarah's desire to leave may have stemmed from their different perceptions of what the city had to offer. From others that had returned to visit family, Sarah knew that Chicago offered independence and material comfort. From talking to these same people, Thurman knew that he would relinquish a certain amount of control of the family and perhaps Sarah. He also knew that, in those terms, there was no going back home.

Sarah was recalling her experience of leaving home while her son, Kenny was present. During the interview he interjected comments into the conversation. From listening to him it was clear that he regretted moving to Chicago. Although just a child when he came, he wondered whether it was worth losing touch with his roots. At one point he stated,

> You come up here to sweat in a steel mill, you don't have any education. See that gentleman who just left? [referring to a man living in the apartment with Sarah] he would go out at three in the morning just to catch a train to 125th Street Stoney Island to go to work, you know just to get by. I think sometimes they should of just sat back in the hills. The last few years I have been back in touch with my grandmother. I went back to Virginia. I would trade any amount of Chicago for a little space back in Virginia some place. [6]

To Kenny there was too much cost associated with moving home. To him losing connection with one's identity was not worth it. In Sarah's mind there was very little choice of whether to leave home. "We couldn't make it down there [West Virginia]. There were no jobs for me no jobs for his father. So we had to come to Chicago." To which Kenny interjected, "Yeah then you fall into a bigger trap. Like I said, go to the record shop and get 'Reading, Writing and Route 22.' "

Often when we think of historical movements of people, the images of particular persons come to mind. Perhaps they are faces from Dorthea Lange photographs, or a movie about migration like *The Grapes of Wrath*. While important and necessary as art, these images influence how we come to understand the mass movement of people. They often leave us with a single impression of the entire migration experience. While art is an important element in capturing an event that stirs our emotion, the finer textures of human relationships and reasons for leaving home are lost, or subsumed under academic jargon. When this happens, diversity and complexity of history remain obscured. The southern migrants who arrived in Uptown roughly between 1950 and 1970 were somewhat more diverse than previous groups of southern migrants to Chicago. Their reasons for coming differed as did their occupational, social and geographic origins. Some left the South to escape abusive relationships, others wanted economic opportunity or adventure. Within families husbands and wives left home for different reasons. Single women like Violet, quoted in the beginning of this chapter, searched for the excitement and glamor mythologized in magazines and exaggerated by those who came back to visit the South. They yearned for better wages, exciting nightlife, and independence that they thought attainable in Chicago. Some left home for no other reason than to join their friends had left previously. Contrary to television depictions like the *Beverly Hillbillies*, not all families arrived in an old jalopy with a generous supply of moonshine. In spite of being portrayed as such in Chicago, not all were destitute mountaineers or misfits. The narratives of the individual migrants speak of the depth of change that migration brought to those who left their homes and settled in Chicago. They shed light on how migration changed their perception of the city, and helps us understand the struggle to survive and adapt in Chicago. The voices of the migrants reveal the personal struggle most experienced after arriving, and capture the disappointment and exhilaration that people lived though. Uncovering the lives of the migrants shows that migration is a human endeavor that people experienced as individuals. I am not implying that larger social and economic changes should not be used or minimized in understanding migration. Push and pull factors are important in understanding the mass exodus of people. In fact these forces were most likely the catalyst or justification for leaving home in the South. They are also an important departure point in understanding the social contours of home.

There were significant structural changes in southern agriculture and mining that propelled migrants northward or at the very least created the option of joining the "hillbilly highway" as the musician Steve Earle termed the northward movement of southerners. Bankruptcy and mechanization forced troubadour Billy Edd Wheeler to leave coal towns. Born in High Coal, West Virginia once a bustling coal camp Wheeler would not recognize it today from the effects of coal industry abandonment. For those who departed more rural agricultural regions of the deep South which experienced the earlier periods of mechanization and the instability of sharecropping, migration bore hope for a better life. Barren land and deserted homesteads that were once occupied by their families are all that remains in some cases. Kicking around his family's homestead today a migrant may unearth a broken bottle that recalls earlier days of familial vitality and community. Yet even in the absence of the physical remnants of home, their words reveal a psychological bond to a place to which many never returned. Home was frozen in time as were the memories created there.

By and large economic conditions played a major role in making migration a necessity. In 1949, family income was less than $2,000 in mountain counties in much of the South. By 1960 little had changed in terms of income. Twenty percent of Kentucky's population had applied for federal relief by 1959.[7] This was the first time that net losses in population were recorded in Kentucky and West Virginia.[8] Officials in the South were aware of population drain as early as the 1940s, but were unable to successfully stem the exodus. The Council of the Southern Mountains (CSM) based at Berea College in Kentucky undertook the task of organizing research, statistics, and conferences on Appalachian migration. The CSM emerged in 1913 to study problems of the Appalachian South. Based in Berea,

Kentucky, the Council had an established record of aiding southerners and tracking the southern out-migration. The Council of the Southern Mountains also organized annual urban migration workshops to unite and inform officials in the North and South about trends in migration.

Population loss in southeastern Kentucky was of grave concern for scholars at the annual CSM conference on urban migration in 1963. Roscoe Giffin, a sociologist at Berea College estimated that over 800,000 people left the counties of the Appalachian South between 1950 and 1956.[9] Between 1950 and 1955, employment in eastern Kentucky coal mines fell from over 47,000 to 25,000, a decline of over 47 percent.[10] Perry County, for example, suffered a loss of 25 percent of its population. In 1950 the population stood at 46,566 and by 1960 the population was 34,961. Other counties experience comparable population declines. Letcher and Breathitt counties lost over 23 and 22 percent of their populations respectively between 1950 and 1960. Leslie County, the birthplace of Raleigh Campbell, who later directed the Chicago Southern Center in Uptown, lost nearly 30 percent of its population during this time. His aunt and family found themselves caught up in the exodus as well. They left for Ohio when he was a young boy. Raleigh's decision to return to Barea College, and his desire to work with migrants in Chicago reflected the profound experience migration had on him as a young boy. It is also important to point out that migration tended to be selective and involved the most capable leaving.[11] It is likely that the population losses would have been greater in light of this fact. Those that remained behind may have been unable to leave.

For many in the South, the future looked bleak. Worn out farms and dying mines characterized many areas. The economic development of the points of origin had proceeded at different paces and had been shaped by technology, main lines of transportation, local geography and natural resources. Therefore eastern Kentucky lost proportionally more residents than western Kentucky, for example. There were significant county variations as well. Not all counties were isolated-mountain hollows. Many of these areas differed in their proximity to larger metropolitan areas in regions experiencing postwar industrial expansion. People in Eastern Kentucky could drive across the Ohio river at many points to work in Cincinnati. In places like Greenville, Tennessee and Abington, Virginia there was beauty, and contentment. Valley counties tended to hold residents better than any areas of the Southern Appalachian region because of industrial development there. In Tennessee Valley Authority developments, population losses were minimal compared to counties such as Clay County, Kentucky, where entire families up and left.[12]

The only two bus companies in Bluefield, West Virginia were selling an average of 100 one-way tickets to Cleveland a week by the late 1950s. When busses were filled drivers pulled extra shifts to accommodate those wishing to leave, and to make extra money. In 1958, the county clerk in Grayson, Kentucky, Clyde Johnson, commented that, "we lose some of our young people but nine-tenths of them come back eventually, that's why we have so much unemployment." A more nostalgic editor of the Grayson newspaper, W. L. Postlewaite, claimed that "most of those who leave here find that they don't like living in the big cities." A more informed minister, Reverend Frank Bradburn, pastor of the East Lafollette (Tennessee) Baptist church, reported: "Year before last (1957) 47 members of my 200 member congregation left for jobs up north. Not one has returned that I know of." Similarly, G.M. Southerland, chief accountant of the Omar mining company in Omar, West Virginia commented that "many have gone to cities like Cleveland to work. Some come home for visits on Weekends, but almost none come back to stay. There's nothing to come back to."[13] A series of divergent opinions about conditions and migrants emerged at their points of origin reflecting both the varied economic development and diverse motivations for migration.

Continued mechanization in farming and mining made many leave for Chicago. Often machines were vilified in culture, and took on lives of their own in local legends like a sinister force chasing people from rural areas toward cities. The introduction of the infamous Joy Loader in coal mining displaced thousands of men from the mining industry by the 1950s. This rather simple device could undercut and gather coal in small spaces at a faster rate without risk of human injury. The impact was felt throughout the early twentieth century reaching a peak in the fifties. Mechanization left chronic unemployment, emptied shops of goods and left people with little hope. Eventually the loader became immortalized in culture. A folk song of the time illustrates the plight of those displaced by the mechanical loaders. Sung in a dreary and pleading tone the words almost beseech a return to the back breaking and dangerous work some compared to slavery:

> Tell me what will a poor miner do?
> Tell me what will a poor miner do?
> When he go down in the mines
>   Joy Loaders he will find
> Tell me what will a poor miner do?
> Miners poor pocketbooks
>   are growing thin.
> Miners poor pocketbooks
>   are growing thin.
> They can't make a dollar at all
>   place it all on that coal loading machine.[14]

Paralleling the structural shifts in the coal industry were dramatic cuts in agricultural workers made redundant by the introduction of machines. Postwar mechanization of cotton harvesting hit hard in the deep south. International Harvester's mechanical cotton picker eliminated millions of agricultural workers. This reduced the number of man hours to produce a bale from 160 to 28. By 1945 this had affected over 2 million workers in the deep south. Between 1950 and 1959 the number of farm production workers declined by 50 percent from 3 million to approximately 1.5 million.[15] While mechanization was profitable for large farmers, small commercial farmers all over the South were unable to compete with the larger mechanized units in the East and the South. The result was a 38 percent decline in small commercial farms between 1950 and 1959.[16] Migrant Mary Woods and her family left Tennessee because of the spread mechanization in farming. Virginia Bowers left Blytheville, Arkansas in 1960 after her husband was injured in an accident with a tractor. She would later become active in the Students for a Democratic Society (SDS) in Chicago. She recalls the human toll mechanization of farming took on people she knew back home, and how few had any choice but to leave.

> The [migrants] didn't have any education. They came off farms. Farming had just got mechanized and a lot of them were sharecroppers. Farms started using machinery and they could have just a few hands to do the farming. There were no factories there where they could go to work. They either had friends here [Chicago] or their families had friends here. My husbands cousins lived around steel plants in Indiana.

Previously, cotton had begun a slow migration west to California ranches driving many off of the former plantations by the end of the 1950s.[17] This was but one in a long series of events that resulted in rural people leaving their homes for cities within the South and other regions of the United States. Laborers, sharecroppers, and their families all found themselves with choices unimaginable in their parents' generation. Though many were poor, the stability gained from several generations on the same land was lost.

By 1963, areas of eastern Kentucky were judged hopeless by a Ford Foundation study. "Famine, geographic isolation, exploitative coal mining, and timbering, and inadequate transportation" were among the problems that characterized the region.[18] The State of Kentucky had long supported the interests of the coal industry at the expense of its residents. This left an underdeveloped infrastructure, poor and inadequate schools, and little fiscal power for local governments. Until 1988, Kentucky was the only major Appalachian coal producing state which prohibited local government from taxing minerals wealth or property, for example. Coal tax revenue was insignificant because the owners of the mineral rights often differed from the land owners who were out of state residents. Those who owned the land were taxed and those who owned the vast mineral wealth were not, leaving a heavier tax burden on those least able to afford it.[19]

Through the 1960s stories emerged of destitute men stealing coal to heat family stoves during the winter. Images were beamed into suburban living rooms of gaunt skeleton-like figures on paint-bare porches with bare foot children clawing at their aprons. National attention was called to the Appalachian South where men with seven children were making fifteen dollars a week chopping wood. Overcrowded shacks stinking of urine, with partially clothed children playing in filth appeared in newspapers throughout America. Pictures of men digging drainage ditches as part of an "aid-to-jobless-fathers" program appeared in the media highlighting the economic realities of home that harked back to the days of the New Deal.[20] Many of these families were simply too poor or too old to leave the South. By this time millions of people with the ability to do so were already in Chicago and other Midwestern cities. These families were Michael Harrington's "other Americans" that influenced the War On Poverty.

Conditions in the South led President John F. Kennedy to appoint the Appalachian Regional Commission to come up with a strategy for the region. During the sixties no less than five congressional enactments were directed at the southern mountains: The Area Redevelopment Act of 1961, The Public Works Acceleration Act of 1962, The Public Works and Economic Development act of 1965, The Appalachian Redevelopment act of 1962, and the Economic Redevelopment Act of 1965. Although the commission proposed a $4.5 billion redevelopment price tag, Congress only appropriated just over a billion for the Appalachian Development Act in 1965. Four fifths of the funds appropriated, however, went to highway construction rather than housing, schools, reforestation, stream cleanup, or other human or environmental projects. The logic behind the act was to aid kick start industry and spur regional economic development without hurting the vested interests of the region. Unfortunately, this strategy probably hastened the exodus of many southerners and left the region economically and environmentally ravaged.[21]

In a stark contrast to rural poverty, national prosperity fueled a postwar housing boom resulting in huge suburbs in Levittown on Long Island in New York and Westwood in Los Angeles. Thousands of houses complete with amenities unknown to many migrants were gradually becoming common place in other regions surrounding major cities. The Interstate Highway Act and huge commuter rail systems made the suburbs more accessible to the majority of those employed in cities. Ironically, the same interstate highways which would evacuate thousands of middle class city dwellers out to the suburbs took thousands of southerners up north to Chicago.

What is not captured in the academic, media and government accounts discussed above are the individuals and families involved in the economic events. As mentioned above, often large movements of people are seen in monolithic terms. When we are confronted with the task of explaining migration, we reduce individuals to trends or statistics or catastrophic events such as the Boll Weevil infestation. Although important, this type of analysis leaves out the complexity involved in the decision to leave home. When discussing the homes and communities they left for Chicago, it is apparent that individuals made up the large exodus of those from the South. When interviewed the migrants' stories reminded me that simple economic factors do not necessarily explain this mass exodus of people from all parts of the South. In spite of the larger forces that made many leave out of economic necessity, I was told of more individualized reasons such as domestic violence or alcoholism. Moreover, their lives show us that it was not easy to leave home. Leaving home was difficult. There was an emotional and psychological cost involved in departure. With their material possessions and photographs, each person carried their memories of home and individual reasons for leaving with them to Chicago. What they say about home reveals the depth of change many experienced once in Chicago, and the opportunity the city offered to escape occupational danger as well as personal entanglements.

Home was both romanticized and despised. Home was the best worst place on earth. It was a place where men dug coal out of a seam in a pall of coal dust to feed their families. If they were lucky enough to be working, they may be digging low coal where most worked crawling or duck-walking in front of a continuous mining machine. Life and work in the mines was brutal and unforgiving. The constant danger in the mines was a particular hardship for mining families. Women continually feared that a fall, electrocution, or gas explosion would kill or maim their loved ones. Because of the hours men worked women worried alone or in the company of other women. Single women were told by their mothers and friends that marrying a miner would almost guarantee widowhood.[22] By 1980, in West Virginia alone thousands of women urged husbands to leave the mines.[23]

The dirty work, and dangerous life served as a backdrop for men of the coal towns. Family life was shaped by the conditions and routine of the coal mines. For women home was a place of anticipatory danger. Ruby grew up and married a miner. Before coming to Chicago she had never traveled away from home except to give birth. Children would have to wait until the weekends to see their father because they left before the kids got up and returned after they'd gone to bed. "Miners came home. They just set their lunch buckets down. They were dirty. Some of them fell asleep right beside the fire. Got up and went back to work."[24] The impact would first be felt by a mother waiting for her husband's return, and then by the daughter who would probably marry a miner. One coal miner's wife had this to say about the relationship between home and mining:

> For days you didn't even see them, you know. It would be dark when they go to work and we'd be in bed when they come home. Sometimes you didn't even see them till Sunday morning. And that was just a way of life for the people in my coal mining community. When I grew up we wasn't living, we was just existing. The best thing that a girl could hope for was to find a boy who had a job to marry and go right back to the same thing that she come out of.[25]

Women suffered psychologically from coal mining. Death haunted families and friends in communities. One way women from mining areas voiced their fear, frustration, and fortitude was through song. The health of their men, the conditions in the mines, the disdain for company bosses, and the dreaded black lung disease were all subjects of songs women wrote in coal mining areas. Some songs like, "Hello Coal Miner" by Sarah Ogan Gunning, allude to a mythology of lung disease, death, and fathers telling their sons never to follow in their foot steps. Songs by women describe the burdens of the miners' wives and children and the longing to escape the drudgery of coal camp life. Starvation, sickness, poor housing, and disease.[26] In 1938 Alvin Carter recorded, "Coal Miner's Blues" which illustrated the fears and hardship of work in the mines. Carter expressed the thoughts of millions regarding their work and those who worried for them. The lyrics allude to the unique nature of mining and the precarious and unstable nature of the work.

> Some blues are just blues, mine are the miner's blues.
> My Troubles are coming by threes and twos
> Blues and more blues, it's that coal black blues.
> Got coal in my hair, got coal in my shoes.
> These blues are so blue they're coal black blues.
> For my place will cave in, and my life I will lose.
> I'm out with these blues dirty coal black blues.
> We'll lay off tomorrow with these coal miners blues.[27]

The long hours and years of employment often ended with an injury or disablement through black lung disease (pneumoconiosis) which took years to show up. This disease is caused when miners breathe fine particles of coal dust suspended in the air in mines. The dust collects in the tiny nodules in the lungs, destroys the lung tissue, impairs the transfer of oxygen to the blood, and leads to an enlargement of the heart and eventual death. Families had entire generations of black lung victims because the disease went undiagnosed for years. It was not until 1969, with the passage of the Federal Coal Mine Health and Safety Act, that the federal government officially recognized pneumoconiosis (black lung) as a compensable occupational disease.[28] This had a direct impact on former miners like Lawrence Zorn in Chicago who cofounded the Chicago Area Black Lung Association aimed at helping those qualified to claim benefits. Sometimes compensation arrived after their husband's death. In one case, a miner had symptoms which were denied by doctors for years until it was too late. The family subsistence was worsened by not having a legitimate claim to benefits, and the company's reluctance to use him in the mines because of his attempt to claim disability. His benefits came through fifteen days after his death.[29]

Other dangers were associated with work in the South. Sarah Dotson was raised by her grandparents. Sarah lost her father when she was sixteen months old, and her mother died when she was thirteen. Her grandmother was a midwife and her grandfather, Will, ran a saw mill. It was not long before she realized the danger associated with logging.

> The last thing I remember him [her grandfather] a doin' He had a sawmill across the creek and he had a big skidway. You don't know what a skidway is I don't guess. And four logs across the creek. And they had to bring those logs, their timber across those logs, across the creek to put them on the truck. And he was doin' that one day and he fell off the skidway and busted himself up you know. So that went down the tubes, he could never do that no more. But he had kids that worked and made money, and he had to turn everything to them. Then he wanted my grandmother to quit running around delivering babies.

In many ways, migrants in Chicago romanticized their homes in the South. Despite the hardship, and lack certain amenities, home was a place that most wanted to return if even only to be laid to rest. When I spoke to Sarah about home in Williamson, West Virginia, she became animated and enthusiastic. When Sarah was young, her house was heated with wood. She had heard that the apartments in Chicago were more comfortable. Steam heat, indoor plumbing and other features of apartments appealed to many female migrants. While sitting with her in Chicago, Sarah, made a point of contrasting the difference between her apartment and her home in West Virginia. In somewhat nostalgic terms, she spoke of what they did without back home. "We had a coal stove. Way in the night the house would get cold. And you'd have to get up and build a fire in the cook stove and the heat stove. Water came from wells and they was always low. Chicago was a place where you could sleep in the winter with only a sheet on the bed."[30] Along with the inconvenience of wood stoves and inadequate plumbing, came difficulty getting to stores because of impassable roads, natural disasters, or the unstable and inadequate income. Most migrants originated in regions characterized by self sufficiency, often out of necessity. Families in these regions had long been independent, and many were subsistence farmers.[31] Trips to the store were reserved for more bulk items such as flour. They had a social dimension as well. Going to the store meant the chance to swap stories and receive news. Sarah's family was no exception. "You raised your own chickens, had your own eggs, your own vegetables. You really didn't have to buy anything at the store . . . just, you know, your lard, your salt, your flour."[32] In Jack Kirby's book *Rural Worlds Lost*, a Clay County West Virginian recalled that people would let their hogs run wild through the woods and used dogs to round them up for fattening and slaughter. Much like Sarah romanticizing her economic hardship, Kirby quoted a West Virginia migrant as saying that families "didn't want for anything to eat in them days."[33]

Domestic violence was a topic most women discussed at some point when recalling home. Gender roles in the South, were often enforced by violence.[34] Women often recalled that they rarely left home except to have children or attend church. Virginia Bowers concealed her pregnancy from her first husband before leaving because of the fear that it might bring on personal repercussions. "I was pregnant when I got my divorce, but I did not tell my husband that the child was his because I knew that I would not have nothing but problems out of it. It got to where he was too mean to me. He used to drink and fight me, you know."[35] Virginia was worried that her husband would use the birth of a child to prevent her from leaving Alabama. In the end, she concealed her pregnancy until the divorce was completed and went to Chicago.

Helen lived under the shadow of alcoholism and instability. She boasted of the advantages of her life in the farming area in which she lived in Tennessee. Though she stated that Tennessee would always be home, she spoke in ambiguous tones about family life in the South. She made a distinction about how life could be in the South, and the life that she endured there. When I interviewed her, she sat in a crowded and dilapidated apartment in Uptown. She characterized her life as being a series of moves within the South until she came to Chicago at age nineteen. She was born into a farming family in Humboldt, Tennessee in the 1940s. Her childhood was characterized by migration within the South. Her mother worked in the fields helping her father, a sharecropper. When Helen was ten her family left Tennessee for Mississippi without her father.

> My dad was a drinker, and he wasn't doing what he was supposed to do. My grandfather came and told him that he was drinking and that he wasn't doing what he was supposed to do. 'You're not taking care of the family. It's time to move on. I'm taking Lily and the three kids with me. You can either come with us and stop drinking or stay here.'[36]

In Mississippi, she began helping her grandfather on a shrimp boat during the summer. A year later her family moved to Florida. In 1967, Helen came to Chicago to join her mother and uncle who owned a bar. Her first apartment was on Montrose Street.

In spite of the independence and economic opportunity that urban life offered, migrants expressed a great fondness for life in the South. Clara remembered the humiliation of being poor, but the closeness of family life, and the importance of religion and spirituality as sustaining people. Moreover, the common class position most occupied helped soften the blow of poverty and bound people together. During one interview Clara pointed out the importance of family, class and kin when she recalled the amount of sharing that went on among people. "It seemed like there was more togetherness at home. It seemed like everybody was on the same level. Didn't no one have too much more than the other. If I ate beans, you ate beans too."[37]A degree of interdependence existed both within the family and among families. Their shared sense of class and cooperation helped many migrants survive in Chicago and led to a common identity. Community was also forged through common experiences. Residents of mining communities shared a common bond that often extended through several generations. Strong emotional ties emerged out of these experiences. The family was typically the center of social interaction, and emotional support. Families pooled their resources to help with funerals, healing, and caring for a newborn or the elderly. The family was often the only thing separating hope from despair.

Religion played a dual role in the lives of the migrants back home. By and large, southern migrants belonged to Baptist congregations or more fundamentalist strains such as the Church of God. Sarah Dotson belonged to the Church of God, but preferred the Baptist services. Religion had both a spiritual and social component which often overlapped. Perhaps more than any other aspect of life, religion was at the core of community interaction. Church socials were a valued activity. Churches would sponsor box suppers, and cake walks for example. When there were revivals, Sarah would attend the entire time. "Sometimes there would be revivals for about two weeks and we would go for the whole two weeks. I liked the singing and preaching, all of it. We was always in Church."[38] Religion represented a unifying experience whereby members of the community worshiped, expressed needs, shared heartache, exchanged news, and met spouses. Many believed in the certainty of God's will and plan for everyone regardless of skill or luck. This faith in the will of God, eased worries and provided temporary relief from the knowledge that many unpredictable dangers awaited loved ones. It also allowed people to cope when misfortune befell them.[39] Religion was a setting for social interaction and companionship. Men met their girl friends and courted their future wives at church events and revivals. When Sarah Dotson thought back on the revivals and dances she had this to say:

> Them's was the best times, you know. We'd go to church, a bunch of us would go to church. That's where we'd meet our boy friends at. Church was at, we'd start about 6:30 and it would end at about 8:30. And by 9:00 us kids would have to be home. My grandparents had this big grand father clock, and I would have to be in the house by the time that clock got through ticking [chiming] nine times, I had to be in that door. So I always was. They wasn't no delaying at the gate or at the door, you had to be inside that door. I don't care if you had a boyfriend out there or what. And I am real thankful for that. Nowadays you can't get them in at twelve o'clock let alone at nine.[40]

Praying together or attending a revival provided social cohesion and common interests. Community support or social standing was always raised with the support of the clergy. Men and women interpreted these arrangements and social events differently and participated in them for varying reasons. A daughter could gain community prominence and recognition by teaching Sunday school, for example. Friday night dances, box suppers, cake walks, Halloween plays, Wednesday night prayer meetings, and revivals were always a part of religious life for those at home. Families spent their free time at church either at a social event or one of the revivals which could last two weeks or more. A man, however, may attend church to regain face or publicly demonstrate his repentance after backsliding. Virginia remembers her father being baptized and the impression it made on her as a child:

> We had this lake or river where we were baptized. And we looked behind us and here comes my father, you know, with a change of clothes under his arm coming to be baptized. It was kind of funny to us, you know, 'cause we didn't think that he had any intention of joining our church. I'll never forget that.[41]

The church created social bonds for a family, and knit them together with a larger community. Women attended church more regularly than men.[42] Once in Chicago, few of those interviewed attended church regularly. Part of this may stem from the lack of churches in Chicago that appealed to migrants. Helen Elam stated that "we never went to church here [Chicago]. We never found a Baptist church to go to. There wasn't any reason to go. There weren't. There were so many ethnic churches here. And the storefront churches, well we knew phonies when we saw them."[43] Helen went on to say that the form and rituals of southern migrants were unwelcomed in Chicago. Although most migrants were deeply spiritual and used biblical references in interviews, none spoke of attending church in Chicago.

All of the migrants that I interviewed spoke of home in similar terms. If there is some particular element of their identity that they all shared it is one that is based in the experience of leaving home behind, and what that meant to them. An idea of home rooted in movement and migration was inclusive in a migrant's identity. As their birthplace, the South was always home to migrants. Although migrants originated in vastly different parts of the South, they were stereotyped as hillbillies once in the North. This hostile reception resulted in a more romanticized version of home than many left. In the process home became singularly similar for all migrants. The longer that they remained in Chicago the more distant friends and kin in the South became. In spite of this, most migrants remained attached to the places they left and wanted to return home someday; if only to be buried.

The purpose of this chapter was to discuss the variety of reasons for coming to Chicago and paint a social and cultural picture of home. I also wanted to show the magnitude of population losses in the South. It is arguable that the economic factors played a large role in people's decision to leave the South. Indeed the loss of population in the South is unexplainable without a discussion of the mechanization of farming or mining. Certainly the massive job losses that occurred in the Rustbelt cities during the 1970s and 1980s had an impact on the rise in joblessness and poverty in central cities. Much of this would affect those migrants in places like Chicago. But citing the statistics on job losses in Chicago does little to help us understand how families responded, or how their lives changed. People like Donald Powell, Ruby Hanks, or Sarah Dotson may have responded to economic hardship by leaving, but for others like Helen Elam or Violet McKnight being employed did not prevent them from leaving the South.

In addition, I wanted to capture the richness of life and the cultural textures of home to show the complexity involved in migration. What made up the decisions to leave a place from which many had never strayed was shaped by men and women interacting along roles often prescribed by friendship and kin networks. The story of the southern migrant exodus also involved how people understood what urban life offered, and how men and women perceived this in different terms. For mothers, Chicago was a place for their children to attend better schools and get better medical care. While many men viewed leaving as an imperative of survival and employment, the attraction for women centered on the freedom it would offer them from isolation and male dominance, and an opportunity to excel independently of their husbands. Chicago became a place where, as a female migrant put it, " I can get a job, go shopping and not have the hills close up on me."[44]

Some men left the South reluctantly because they were uncertain about their ability to prosper in Chicago. For married men, this meant an added burden to sustain their family in a much more competitive environment having limited skills. Leaving home also meant more of a commitment for those with families. As a result there was more risk involved because there was more to lose. For single men, Chicago was viewed as an adventure which could be easily exchanged for life back home on the weekends. There was little risk in driving to Chicago with friends to work for several months.

Although there was great diversity among the migrants before they left, certain common threads united them once in Chicago. Individual experiences show the southern migrants diversity and individuality. However, a primary element in the minds of migrants is the idea of home. Home became salient in the minds of the migrants. Though from different places home as an idea became similar. Home shaped their recollection of the migration experience because it involved a comparison with Chicago. Although not idyllic and often dangerous for some, home was literally a point of origin. It was where they began, and where important structures of morality and behavior were established. Moreover, home was a place where many wanted to return after they died. Most southern migrants never considered their southern origins until they came to Chicago.

Notes

1. Personal interview by the author with Violet McKnight, 22 June 1994.

2. Personal interview by the author with Sarah Dotson, 20 June 1994.

3. On the African-American experience see for example James Grossman, *Land of Hope: Chicago, Black Southerners and the Great Migration* (Chicago: University of Chicago Press, 1989). For an Okie example see, James Gregory, *American Exodus: The Dust Bowl Migration and Okie Culture in California* (New York: Oxford University Press, 1989). For general discussions of southern labor and migration see, Jacqueline Jones, *The Dispossessed: America's Underclasses from the Civil War to the Present* (New York: Basic Books, 1992); Jack Temple Kirby, *Rural Worlds Lost: The American South, 1920–1960* (Baton Rouge: Louisiana State University Press, 1987), Chad Berry, *Southern Migrants, Northern Exiles* (Chicago: University of Illinois Press, 2000).

4. Migration and women are discussed in the following works: Robert Coles, *The South Goes North* (Boston: Little Brown, 1971), Kathy Kahn, *Hillbilly Women* (Garden City: Doubleday, 1973). Recent attempts have been made to give voice to women in Appalachian history. See for example Betty Jean Hall, "Women Miners Can Dig It Too!" in John Gaventa, Barbara Ellen Smith and Alex Willingham, eds., *Communities in Economic Crisis: Appalachia and the South* (Philadelphia: Temple University Press, 1990).

5. For an extended discussion of this see, Barbara Ellen Smith, " Walk Ons in the Third Act: The Role of Women in Appalachian Historiography," *Journal of Appalachian Studies* 4 (Spring 1998): 5–28.

6. Personal interview by the author with Kenny Dotson, 20 June 1994.

7. Wayne Flynt, *Dixie's Forgotten People* (Bloomington: Indiana University Press, 1978), 141–144.

8. Thomas Ford, ed., *The Southern Appalachian Region: A Survey* (Lexington: University of Kentucky Press, 1962).

9. "Newcomers from the Southern Mountains," in *Cultural Patterns of Newcomers: Selected Papers* (Unpublished report by Chicago Commission on Human Relations, March 1957),16.

10. *Economic Data on Eastern Kentucky Coal Fields.*(Agricultural and Development Board of Kentucky, April 1956), 23.

11. "Exodus from the Hills," *Hazard Herald*, 28 February1963.

12. James S. Brown. "Migration Within To and From the Southern Appalachians, 1935–1959: A Preliminary Report on the Southern Appalachian Studies Migration Project" (Report presented at workshop in Berea Kentucky, 28 September 1959).

13. "Coal Industry Decline Sends Southerners Here," Taken from undated article transcriptions collected by the Council of the Southern Mountains between 1958 and 1960. Southern Appalachian Archives, Berea College.

14. Taken from the film, *Long Journey Home.* Appleshop, Whitesburg, Kentucky, 1991.

15. Donald B. Dodd and Wynelle S. Dodd, *Historical Statistics of the South, 1790-1970* (Birmingham: University of Alabama, 1973).

16. Flynt, *Dixie's Forgotten Poeple*, 96–98.

17. Kirby, *Rural Worlds Lost*, 75–79.

18. "Eastern Kentucky Called Hopeless." *Louisville Times*, 25 November 1963.

19. Gaventa, Smith, and Willingham, *Communities in Economic Crisis.*

20. "Downhill Town," *Louisville Courier-Journal*, 10 June, 1965.

21. Flynt, *Dixie's Forgotten People*, 141–144.

22. Carol A. B. Giesen, *Coal Miners' Wives: Portraits of Endurance* (Lexington: The University Press of Kentucky, 1995), 46.

23. West Virginia State Government, *Annual Report and Directory of Mines, 1986.* Official statistics indicate that between 1897 and 1939, 346 men a year died in the mines. Between 1939 and 1980 that figure fell to 146 per year. It should not be assumed that this reduction was due to increased safety, alone. There had been a steady and significant reduction in the labor force during this time.

24. Mike Yarrow, "Voices from the Coal Fields," in Gaventa, Smith and Willingham, *Communities in Economic Crisis.*

25. Quoted from a migrant, Julia Cowens, in the film, *Long Journey Home* (Appleshop, Whitesberg, Ky, 1991).

26. Henrietta Yurchenco, "Trouble in the Mines, a History of Song and Story of Women in Appalachia," *American Music* (Summer 1991): 209–224.

27. Flynt, *Dixie's Forgotten People*, 161.

28. David E. Whisnant, *Modernizing the Mountaineer* (Boone, N.C.:Appalachian Consortium Press, 1980),161.

29. Giesen, *Coal Miners' Wives*, 60.

30. Personal interview by the author with Sarah Dotson, 20 June 1994.

31. Kirby, *Rural Worlds Lost*, 46–48.

32. Sarah Dotson interview, September 8, 1994.

33. Kirby, *Rural Worlds Lost*, 46.

34. Patricia Gagne, "Appalachian Women: Violence and Social Control." *Journal of Contemporary Ethnography* 20, No. 4 (January 1992): 387–415

35. Personal interview with Virginia Bowers, March 18, 1994.

36. Personal interview with Helen Elam, December 18, 1994.

37.Julia Cowens in the Film, "Long Journey Home."

38. Personal interview with Sarah Dotson September 8, 1994.

39. Scott, "Where There is No Middle Ground."

40. Sarah Dotson interview, September 8, 1994

41. Personal interview by the author with Virginia Bowers, March 18, 1994.

42. Bowers interview.

43. Personal Interview by the author with Helen Elam, December 18, 1994.

44. Elam interview.

Chapter 2

Destination Uptown: A Rocky Evolution

Uptown, Chicago, which at its beginning was distinctly rural, changed rapidly until it is now one of the most cosmopolitan districts in the city.[1]

I saw these big apartment buildings and beautiful homes, for which there were no longer seven or eight-children families, cut up so that they could accommodate married couples or single, male or female. There has been a steady disintegration and we have reached out as the main transient area, I think in the whole city of Chicago.[2]

You see, Wilson and Broadway was worse than any southern town because you had the roughest mother fuckers from every small town come up here. They all came to Uptown. So you had the baddest of the bad in one place.[3]

When Sarah Dotson arrived in Uptown in 1959 the image of Uptown as "Hillbilly Heaven" had begun to take hold among Chicagoans. By the time Donald Powell arrived from Tuscaloosa in 1964 the image was fully established. Although only seventeen, he knew about the bars on Wilson Avenue. Like so many other southerners in Uptown, Donald's mother lived in an overcrowded apartment that had been cheaply converted. Like the Irish before them, and Asian and Latino immigrants today, southern migrants accepted their new accommodations with the hope of something better in the future. Though often substandard, the housing suited these newcomers from the South. Donald didn't mind the apartment as much as the man living with his mother. The blighted conditions that made it a port of entry had accelerated when southerners arrived in large numbers making their association with neighborhood decline inevitable. This chapter will discuss the historical evolution of Uptown, and explain how it evolved as a port of entry for southern whites.

Uptown's housing stock played a large role in attracting southern migrants. The large aging buildings, inexpensive rent, and one room apartments made area a logical port of entry for groups with limited resources. During the 1950s and 1960s thousands of southern whites like the Belchers, and the Dotsons settled in Uptown drawn to the same cheap housing that the reform groups sought to eliminate as part of a campaign to eradicate urban decay. Eventually the efforts of conservation groups reduced some of the overcrowded and substandard housing in Uptown.

However, the age of the housing stock, and the steady influx of migrants exacerbated problems in the area and put them on a collision course with long time residents and conservation groups. As new arrivals in cities forced to live in the most affordable housing, southern whites became associated with the cause of neighborhood decline. Like so many others before them southerners were but another scapegoat for the neighborhood conditions.[4]

Today Uptown remains a port of entry. Following the arrival of southern whites, Native Americans came to Uptown along with Puerto Ricans. In the 1970s Latinos and African Americans moved in attracted by the cheap and public housing. In the 1980s and 1990s, refugees from Southeast Asia and the former Soviet Union settled along with hundreds of de-institutionalized mentally ill. More recently urban professionals escaping higher priced property in other neighborhoods have begun to take advantage of a growing sector of condominiums. There is even a growing sector of Uptown that Nigerians occupy. This somewhat exemplifies the fluidity of change that has characterized the community. Long time residents and observers speak of Uptown as "coming up" or "going down." Uptown is a microcosm of postmodern urban life. It is a mosaic of humanity with strands of the roaring twenties, the Reagan revolution, and the Millennium generation. Walking along Broadway and Lawrence today you are as likely to cross paths with an immigrant from Durango, Mexico as you are a punk heading to a show in the Rivera Theater. It is contested terrain that remains in a state of flux. Understanding this port of entry's continuity, and how it has changed requires an examination of the past.

Uptown as a community began to develop long before the formal annexation by Chicago in 1889. The community area of Uptown comprises several older neighborhoods which were once a part of the town of Lakeview. Until 1980 the community area known as Uptown spread as far north as Devon Avenue, encompassing community areas, 3 and 77 (Map 2.1). Today, Uptown is much smaller than its original designation. (Map 2.2). Its Northern border is now marked at Foster Avenue and the southern limit is Irving Park Avenue. The Western portion includes Ravenswood Avenue and the community extends to Lake Michigan on the east. These were natural boundaries which contributed to the evolution of Uptown as somewhat isolated from nearby areas.

Uptown developed independently from the Loop and became a self-contained community by the early twentieth century. Up until the middle of the nineteenth century most of the area remained mostly prairie, forest and swampland. The early farms were mostly in the hands of Swedish and German immigrants. The area just north of Uptown known as Andersonville is still known for a Swedish bakery and restaurant. Recently the area has experienced an influx of more affluent residents because of the conversion of the spacious three-flat building to condominiums. East of Clark Street Andersonville is as close to a suburban neighborhood as a city gets. There are older single family homes and spacious yards for children. It is also off-limits to the poor due of the property values. Because Chicago was built in an east-west axis, the northern part of Chicago grew relatively later than the west or south

Map 2.1
Community Areas of Chicago

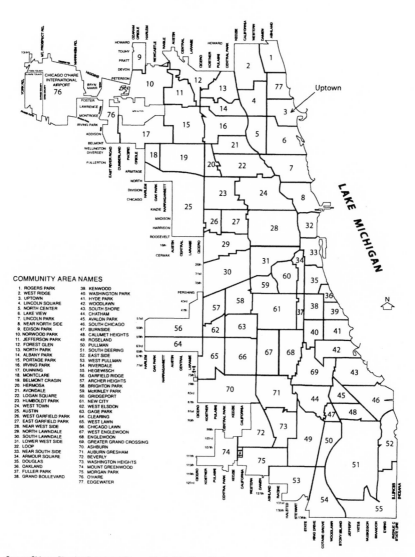

COMMUNITY AREA NAMES

1. ROGERS PARK
2. WEST RIDGE
3. UPTOWN
4. LINCOLN SQUARE
5. NORTH CENTER
6. LAKE VIEW
7. LINCOLN PARK
8. NEAR NORTH SIDE
9. EDISON PARK
10. NORWOOD PARK
11. JEFFERSON PARK
12. FOREST GLEN
13. NORTH PARK
14. ALBANY PARK
15. PORTAGE PARK
16. IRVING PARK
17. DUNNING
18. MONTCLARE
19. BELMONT CRAGIN
20. HERMOSA
21. AVONDALE
22. LOGAN SQUARE
23. HUMBOLDT PARK
24. WEST TOWN
25. AUSTIN
26. WEST GARFIELD PARK
27. EAST GARFIELD PARK
28. NEAR WEST SIDE
29. NORTH LAWNDALE
30. SOUTH LAWNDALE
31. LOWER WEST SIDE
32. LOOP
33. NEAR SOUTH SIDE
34. ARMOUR SQUARE
35. DOUGLAS
36. OAKLAND
37. FULLER PARK
38. GRAND BOULEVARD

39. KENWOOD
40. WASHINGTON PARK
41. HYDE PARK
42. WOODLAWN
43. SOUTH SHORE
44. CHATHAM
45. AVALON PARK
46. SOUTH CHICAGO
47. BURNSIDE
48. CALUMET HEIGHTS
49. ROSELAND
50. PULLMAN
51. SOUTH DEERING
52. EAST SIDE
53. WEST PULLMAN
54. RIVERDALE
55. HEGEWISCH
56. GARFIELD RIDGE
57. ARCHER HEIGHTS
58. BRIGHTON PARK
59. McKINLEY PARK
60. GRIDGEPORT
61. NEW CITY
62. WEST ELSDON
63. GAGE PARK
64. CLEARING
65. WEST LAWN
66. CHICAGO LAWN
67. WEST ENGLEWOOD
68. ENGLEWOON
69. GREATER GRAND CROSSING
70. ASHBURN
71. AUBURN GRESHAM
72. BEVERLY
73. WASHINGTON HEIGHTS
74. MOUNT GREENWOOD
75. MORGAN PARK
76. O'HARE
77. EDGEWATER

Source: Chicago Planning Department (Prepared by Yoshiko Okano Guy)

30

Map 2.2
Uptown

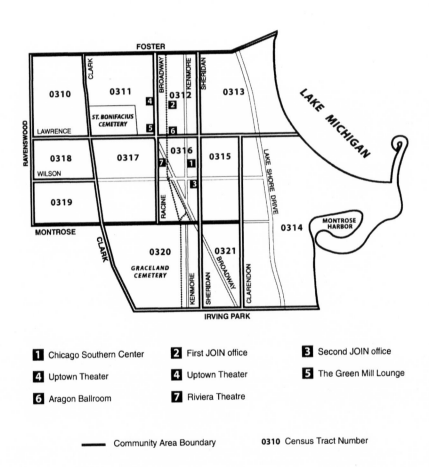

1 Chicago Southern Center	**2** First JOIN office	**3** Second JOIN office
4 Uptown Theater	**4** Uptown Theater	**5** The Green Mill Lounge
6 Aragon Ballroom	**7** Riviera Theatre	

———— Community Area Boundary   **0310** Census Tract Number

Source: Chicago Planning Department (Prepared by Yoshiko Okano Guy)

sides of the city. Transportation was hindered by the Chicago river. Uptown experienced a boom after the Chicago fire of 1871 when the axis of the city changed to north-south. This began a steady movement of people northward away from the city's commercial district. Movement was intensified by the replacement of housing with businesses in the central city. [5]

By the turn of the century, Uptown was out of reach financially to most classes. The first property to be subdivided was Buena Park located between Irving Park, Montrose, Clarendon and Sheriden. Buena Park was home to fairly wealthy people including the children's poet Eugene Field.[6] As late as 1889, most of Uptown had no rail stops. This same year Uptown was annexed by Chicago. Like so many other parts of the country Uptown grew rapidly as rail lines reach outward limits of Chicagoland, and spurred the growth of suburbia. This occurred in Uptown first along the Chicago and Milwaukee railroad line. Some have argued that this was a search for utopia on the part of those benefitting from industrial economic success in cities. The growth of the middle class and search for a more pastoral ideal of a previous landed gentry in England drove the growth, shape, and form of newly emerging suburbs in the United States. Planners like Frederick Law Olmsted, poets like Ralph Waldo Emerson and writers like Catherine Beecher had previously planted in the American consciousness utopian visions of suburbia. This is evident in the development Buena Park, when Swedish immigrants sold their farms to make way for the elegant single family homes. It was the pursuit of a dream home and image of life as the middle class envisioned. The expanding frontier became the periphery of cities like Chicago because the land was cheap and relatively undeveloped.[7] Buena Park was not unlike other initial developments in early suburbs that contained elements of the county and city. It was a place where those able to do so could sequester themselves from urban congestion and the lower classes. It was a place where Eugene Field could be inspired to write the poem, "The Delectable Ballad of the Waller Lot" about the Waller grounds near his home.

Up yonder in Buena Park
There is a famous spot,
In legend and in history
Yclept the Waller Lot.

There children play in daytime
And lovers stroll by dark,
For 't is the goodliest trysting-place
In all Buena Park.

Once on a time that beauteous maid,
Sweet little Sissy Knott,
Took out her pretty doll to walk
Within the Waller Lot.

While thus she fared, from Ravenswood

Came Injuns o'er the plain,
And seized upon that beauteous maid
And rent her doll in twain.[8]

The first four stanzas of the poem revel an idyllic country setting characteristic of early visions of suburbia and impending danger from the frontier. Today this pastoral ideal is increasingly marketed to those less fortunate in the form of modular and mobile homes in rural areas, and cheaply constructed "McMansions" in the exurbs. In Uptown, the opening of the Ravenswood station at Wilson Avenue, and another at Foster Avenue in 1900 spurred considerable development.[9] Between 1910 and 1920 the population in Uptown increased by 45 percent from 44,582 to 89,582. By 1914, most of the vacant land in Uptown was occupied by commercial or residential property. Land owners began to take advantage of the influx of new middle class residents and the concurrent rise in land values. Property was either subdivided or larger residences converted to smaller units. Many residents from more crowded parts of the city were coming to Uptown seeking a more residential life style.[10]

Rail stops and more affordable housing made Uptown desirable to young married couples seeking close proximity to the central city. Unable to keep pace with this demand many older buildings were converted to rooming houses. The "one room apartment" made its debut on Wilson Avenue in 1916.[11] The conversion of large apartment houses led many original residents to migrate further north to Andersonville. One citizen described his impression of this process in early part of the century:

> When I first came to Wilson Avenue, it was a lovely district; all residences, lovely homes and a business district on Broadway. Good apartment buildings were found among the homes until 1910, although by that time people were moving out of the district because they thought that it was beginning to deteriorate. By 1912 and 1913 cheaper apartment houses were built everywhere and many desirable people moved farther north.[12]

Paralleling this residential and transportation growth was a fledgling commercial and entertainment center. By the late 1920s Uptown theaters were nationally known. The Wilson Avenue shopping district eventually competed with the Loop. Businesses clustered around the Wilson Avenue elevated station.[13] At one time Uptown had more delicatessens and sold more cigarettes and candy per capita than any other district in the city of Chicago.[14] The identity of Uptown was being formed during this time. Uptown was not simply a convenient commercial district in close proximity to residents of the Northside. By 1921, it had a solid reputation as a center of retail and entertainment to rival the Loop.[15] It was during this period, the commercial heart of Uptown emerged. During the early part of the century the word, Uptown was first used to describe the area. One store, (Loren Miller and Company) familiarly termed the "Uptown Store" by its owner, Loren Miller, an aggressive and innovative retailer. Among other things he was the first to employ bargain pricing and generous advertising in newspapers. Miller was able to take advantage of the influx of new residents and demand for home furnishing brought on by the housing boom. Instead traveling to the Loop young residents could shop in their own neighborhood. Miller had previously built a prominent five-story building at Lawrence and Broadway in the first of two retail expansions that would make him the most recognizable retail centers in Uptown. Miller believed that the term Uptown would lure more retail and entertainment investment to the area.[16] Local businessmen formally adopted the term, "Uptown" in lieu of the "Wilson Avenue District" in 1921. Miller was an important booster of Uptown and made important strides in heightening the profile of the area. The term suggests its location north of the Loop, as well as the commercial competition it posed for retailers there. This is an important distinction to make because there were no other similar districts in the city during this time. During the 1920s Wilson Avenue, which would later be filled with seedy bars and transient hotels, became the primary commercial center of the area. Commercial expansion of this district was given a boost after World War II when street lighting along Broadway from Lawrence to Sunnyside was constructed.[17] Until 1950, Uptown merchants had higher retail sales and more floor space than the Loop.[18] Loren Miller and Company was bought by the Goldblatt brothers in 1931 whose Goldblatt's department stores offered consumers cheap mass produced goods. The Goldblatt's store remained as an important discount retail anchor in Uptown throughout the twentieth century. The Uptown Goldblatt's was the last to close, remaining in operation until 1988.

Throughout the early twentieth century Uptown remained one of the most popular retail, commercial, and residential centers in Chicago. Uptown reached a commercial and residential zenith between 1925 and 1942.[19] Previously the Clark Street streetcar line had been extended north through the area to join a newly opened street car line east and west along Lawrence Avenue. Suburban rail and the elevated trains cut commuting times to other parts of the city. Rapid transit lured new residents with promises of affordable housing and unlimited economic possibilities regardless of status.[20] Though the new transportation made Uptown a desirable place to live, it also meant an increase in property taxes and real estate costs, and ripe for speculators. Eventually many of the older mansions were sold and replaced by expansive towering apartment hotels like the Sheridan Plaza, the Chelsea, the Lawrence, and the infamous Leland. Most of these hotels ranged from eight to twelve stories and were built within ten years of one another. Most of these hotels offered weekly, monthly and daily rates and appealed to single men and women who were new to Chicago. Eventually these prestigious hotels would be abandoned by residents for the suburbs and attract transients, degenerates or be converted to SROs (single room occupancy) and sheltered care facilities for the mentally ill and elderly of Uptown. In the 1990s, while conducting research for this, I canvassed residents, who resided in these former hotels. Most were filled with the urban poor and elderly. They were dark and dangerous firetraps.

Uptown also had a vibrant night life. To the dismay of some, Uptown was also rapidly becoming an adult entertainment Mecca. Movie theater capacity ranked second only to the loop.[21] Adding to prestige and popularity of the area was the location of Essany studios on Argyle Street. One of the first ballrooms to open was the Arcadia on Broadway in 1910. Serving as a dance hall and skating rink, the Arcadia was extremely popular with residents of Uptown as well as other parts of the city. The Arcadia and the Green Mill Gardens were unique in that white audiences could see all black jazz groups. Therefore, the Arcadia tended to attract a younger crowd in search eclectic dance styles and members of the opposite sex. The popularity was eventually eclipsed by the opening of the Aragon in 1926. In 1950 the building was destroyed by fire.[22]

Although the Wilson and Riviera theaters were popular, the Uptown theater, built in 1925, became an architectural landmark rivaled in size only by Radio City Music Hall. Located at 4816 North Broadway it measured over 46,000 square feet, seated 4,027 and contained a jewelry shop, drug store, shoeshine stand, and the Montmartre night club. One long-time resident reminisced about sneaking into the Uptown and the Riviera theaters during the thirties:

> Friday night was Uptown theater night for us. It had fire exit doors leading to Magnolia Street, and once we discovered a way to open them from the outside we enjoyed movies and stage shows for no cost. We did not fare so well at the Riviera. One night [we] entered it by climbing a fire escape leading to the men's room. A suspicious usher spotted us in the lobby and asked for our ticket stubs. My fast thinking brother told him that we had thrown them away. The usher then informed us that they didn't issue stubs. This ended our forays into the Riviera.[23]

Uptown's reputation as a center entertainment and night life was boosted by its numerous ballrooms built during the 1920s and 1930s. The Karzas brothers built the Aragon Ballroom in 1926 on the corner of Lawrence and Broadway. At a cost of $1,750,000, the Aragon resembled a Moorish palace with imitation twinkling stars set the tone for romantic dancing.[24] Unlike most other ballrooms of the time, the Aragon enforced strict dress codes, high standards of behavior, and prohibitions close dancing and jitterbugging. As a result, it tended to attract older, middle and upper class patrons. The youth preferred the Green Mill Gardens or the Arcadia for jazz.[25] Legend has it that tunnels that lead from the Aragon to the Green Mill. The Green Mill Gardens on Broadway at Lawrence was noted for stand-up comedy and musical acts. Opened in 1914, the Green Mill was one of the most popular jazz spots in Uptown. Comedian Joe E. Lewis was one of the comedians working the Green Mill in 1927. When Al Capone heard that Lewis had accepted a job at a rival bar across the street, his men intervened and the "young comedians face never looked the same."[26] Today the Green Mill is featured in movies, and frequented by an esoteric mix of patrons who listen to live jazz after midnight, poetry slams, or attend punk shows at the nearby Aragon Ballroom.

By the Depression, Uptown had begun to change from an upscale commercial and entertainment district to an area known for vice due in part to the growth of the skin trade earlier. These seeds of decline were built into Uptown's success as an entertainment district. The mushrooming night club industry and the influx of visitors presented a lucrative opportunity for vice, cheap hotels, and clip joints.[27] In addition more people were living in Uptown. The previous construction of large hotels, and unchecked conversion of apartments to smaller units resulted in a burgeoning population often in overcrowded and unsafe buildings. As a result, rental property had begun to dominate dwelling units in the area. By 1940 Uptown was one of the most densely populated community areas in the city with over 12,500 people per square mile.[28] Surveys done by the W.P.A. (Works Progress Administration) indicated that the area between Irving Park and Montrose Avenues, had the largest concentration of rooming houses in the Chicago with 10 or more units per block; fertile ground for a port of entry.[29]

There were other indicators that Uptown was entering a cycle of decline. As early as 1930 less than 6 percent of the dwelling units in Uptown were owner occupied. Most of these were on the east side in an elite enclave along Lake Michigan.[30] Moreover, many of the dwelling units were aging large apartments for four or more residents.[31] During World War II, absentee landlords continued to divide up these large apartment houses into kitchenettes first to accommodate women of servicemen seeking close proximity to the Great Lakes Navel base. Just one rail stop away, the base added a rough element to the area. Drunken brawls were becoming commonplace along Wilson Avenue. Military Police were regularly at the railroad station in Uptown to control rowdy G.I.'s Many of these conversions were hastily done for profit. This added to Uptown's reputation as a shabby area of one room kitchenettes and transients.

When large numbers of southern migrants began to arrive in 1950s Uptown was a very different place than it had been in the 1920s. Median income and education of residents had declined. The number of residents reporting "no school years completed" increased 89 percent from 395 in 1950 to 750 in 1960. Uptown was also becoming a blue collar neighborhood. Between 1950 and 1960 the percentage of blue collar workers surpassed white collar workers. By 1960, blue collar workers made up more than 50 percent of the total employed living in Uptown.[32] Two factors may account for this: The aging housing stock, cheap rent, and general decline of the area drove white collar workers out and attracted blue collar workers. Owner-occupied housing declined between 1950 and 1960 in all census tracts. In some tracts less than 2 percent of the housing was owner-occupied by 1960.[33] This was also driven by expanding suburbs in the United States during the immediate postwar period. Beginning in 1950 census data revealed that most inner cities in the U.S. experienced net losses of population for the next thirty years. During this same period, the suburban population more than doubled, leaving behind a wasteland of urban decay. The continued suburban exodus depressed the prices of older housing stock in cities as a chase for newer homes ensued. The reuse of residential property in America is characterized by the occupancy of progressively lower income groups.[34] This national trend was reflected in Uptown as well. Between 1950 and 1960, property values fell as much as 26 percent in some census tracts.[35] Uptown's vacancy rate in 1960 was 25 percent (double that of the overall city rate) for one-room and two-room units, which made up over 50 percent of the total housing. Much of this housing was the elegant hotels which had begun to fall into disrepair. Officials were alarmed at the mass conversions of large apartments to rooming houses. As early as the 1940s local officials and business leaders expressed concern over mass evictions and rising rents. In 1951, Alderman Allan A. Freeman of the 48th ward (Uptown) introduced an ordinance which required landlords to obtain approval from the City Council to break up apartments into smaller units. Freeman attributed the "slum conditions" in Uptown to the growing practice of "indiscriminate conversions for profit." He also believed that this was accelerating the exodus of families to the suburbs. Tenants were evicted and large apartments were rapidly converted to smaller units.[36] Most of the conversions, according to Freeman, were performed in violation of building codes, resulting in unsanitary and dangerous conditions for residents. Added to this were large numbers of unpaved alleys neglected by the city for years. The ordinance would also require landlords to go before a zoning board and conduct public hearings before requesting approval from the City Council. The ordinance got a boost less than a month later when three children were killed in an apartment blaze.[37] Opponents of the ordinance argued that it would only lead to more illegal conversions, and that time was needed to study it. This infuriated Freeman and other aldermen who argued that officials were simply stalling to take the side of landlords.[38]

Moreover, surveys showed that between 1950 and 1960 the Broadway-Lawrence shopping district fell from first to ninth in retail trade from the Loop to Evanston.[39] The trend that was echoed throughout the nation during this period as major retailers experienced sharp declines in sales. The expanding suburbs far from the inner cities contained willing consumers who preferred stores in the suburbs which were less congested and more accessible by auto. The retail slump was felt more by large department store whose clients tended to be middle-class shoppers. More and more residents of inner cities did not have the income to support department stores like Marshall Field's.[40] Moreover, the new construction of larger homes in the suburbs required the purchase kitchen appliances like washers and home necessities like televisions. Southerners both black and white entering cities during in the postwar era arrived in the midst of a retail crisis that would only be solved by stores slowly evacuating to suburban locations. Moreover, public policy such as the Interstate Highway Act not only affected the development of suburbs, but resulted in the decline of urban hotels by offering more ways to bypass cities.[41]

These national trends did not escape public notice in Uptown. Newspaper headlines proclaimed that blight was invading the city creating slums in Uptown. In his inaugural speech in 1947 Mayor Kennelly promised that housing, school and transportation would be his first order of business.[42] In 1952, Kennelly unveiled a city-wide program for alleviating blight. The mayor was already credited with reducing crime, prostitution and, implementing school reform in the city. Kennelly would later lose the mayoral race to Richard Daley in 1955.[43] Kennelly's

Commission on Neighborhood Conservation, cited a report that showed more than 25 percent of the buildings in Uptown were on the verge of serious decay. The commission outlined recommendations for neighborhood improvement, and allocated limited funds to accomplish it. The rest of the money would come from federal funding available to cities for slum clearance. Under Title I of the Wagner, Ellender, Taft Housing Act of 1949, federal funds would cover up to two-thirds of the costs incurred by a local government in the purchase and clearance of blighted sights designated as conservation areas. The problem for the Commission on Neighborhood Conservation was the clause in Title I which called for clearance and construction of residential tracts rather than conversion and renovation. As a result the plan for conservation would stall until local groups spearheaded efforts to improve dilapidated housing and overcrowding in Uptown.[44] Much of this blighted housing was occupied by recent newcomers from the South. This would set the stage for a battle of affordable housing that continues today.

The Uptown Chicago Commission (UCC) took over efforts at neighborhood conservation in 1955. The UCC's mission was to improve the quality of life for Uptown residents by focusing on safety, community development, and land use. Bank presidents, developers, and real estate executives led this organization. Edward E. Dobbeck, vice president of the Uptown National Bank, was the first president of the UCC. Dobbeck was the former director of the Uptown Chamber of Commerce, and had a proven record of fund raising.[45] The UCC had clear ties with the newly elected Mayor, Richard Daley. The wife of Daley's city planner Ira Bach served on the board of the UCC.[46] The UCC was concerned that neighborhood decline would erode land values, the tax base which would affect the residential and commercial base of Uptown. Local forces ran into the same problem as those in City Hall did previously. Federal funding would not be available for the reconversion of one-room apartments, junk car removal, code, enforcement or neighborhood conservation which Uptown desperately needed. As a result, local leaders called for public-private cooperation with home owners to bear the brunt of funding neighborhood conservation.[47] Dobbeck was able to raise $15,000 during the first year and set goal of $25.000 for the UCC's second year,1957. Because individual families made up the bulk of those giving money, Dobbeck's second goal was to increase the membership of the UCC. The low rate of owner-occupied units in many areas of Uptown made this difficult and limited to more affluent families.[48]

The interests of a small number of homeowners, politicians, and business in Uptown coincided. As in any local movement, political and entrepreneurial support was a great advantage. This made it far easier to work within "the system." In this way, residents were able to mobilize a full range of communication, social control, and official support for their goals. The UCC was concerned about a decline in property values which threatened loans held by the Uptown National Bank. As an alternative to federal funding, the UCC pressured city inspectors to enforce code violations, and advocated the reconversion of rooming houses to apartments. The group reported substandard housing and overcrowding to city inspectors. Following this, violations were filed against the owners resulting in fines or conversions.[49] In one case, 82 people were found in a building with 31 single rooms. Garbage violations, faulty stairways, missing fire extinguisher, and the "failure to maintain certified clerks for the hotel-type buildings" were among the violations.[50]

Wilson Avenue was seen as a key sector in neighborhood improvement. As an anchor to the major shopping corridor Wilson Avenue off of Broadway continued to be a nest of firetrap hotels, one room kitchenettes, and seedy bars. Most despised by the UCC was the Wilson Club Hotel owned by Sam Koppel and Sam Rosen, both Democratic precinct captains which meant they were protected by city hall. After multiple continuances a court order was issued forcing them to install a sprinkler system in the hotel.[51] Some progress was made when the executive director of the UCC, Albert N. Votaw announced that owners of rooming houses were beginning to restoring single rooms in their buildings to unfurnished apartments. In some cases, they were being forced to do so after their buildings were found to be in violation of building codes. In other cases the owners were voluntarily considering de-conversion to attract more families and stable tenants. Rather than furnished units rented without a lease, Votaw urged owners rent unfurnished apartments with leases to deter a transient population. Mush of this improvement in housing was attributed to strict enforcement of new housing codes by teams of inspectors in Uptown. These efforts by the UCC were somewhat successful. The number of rooms occupied by more than one person declined by 36 percent during this period. The percentage substandard housing declined from 27 percent to 21 percent between 1950 and 1960.[52] Overall, Uptown was still very much troubled by substandard housing (figure 2.1). Over sixty percent of the housing was still substandard in certain census tracts in 1960. Building owners often avoided violations by setting up model apartment at code to show inspectors in order to get the rest of the building passed. A manager was told to show inspectors the model and claim the entire building was identical. The inspectors accepted this often without verifying by checking other apartments.[53]

The UCC believed that code enforcement alone would not halt the growth of slums.[54] The Commission requested $3 million dollars in 1957 from the Community Conservation Board (the city arm of federal disbursement) to carry out major neighborhood renovations, an Uptown face lift. Improvements included razing buildings for parks and schools, and the creation of residential islands by closing off streets.[55] By including slum clearance newly elected UCC president, Albert Votaw hoped to tap into the federal matching funds under Title I of the Wagner, Ellender, Taft Housing Act of 1949.[56] The city rejected the UCC plan for urban renewal. The Community Conservation Board decided to funnel the federal money to other neighborhoods in Chicago. (Although by 1958 Chicago ranked second in net urban renewal capital grants disbursed ($13,723,422), most of it went to the South and Near West sides. Tensions ran high between the UCC and the Community Conservation Board. The UCC felt that the projects they proposed

Figure 2.1
Substandard Housing in Uptown
1950 and 1960

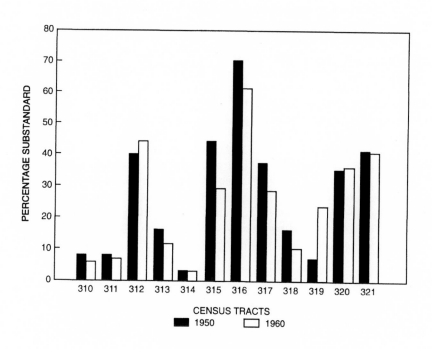

Source: U.S. Bureau of the Census, Seventeenth Census of the United States. "General
Characteristics of the Population by Census Tracts, 1950" (Washington, D.C.: General
Printing Office 1953) U.S. Bureau of the Census, Eighteenth Census of the United
States. "Social Characteristics of the Population by Census Tracts, 1960" (Washington,
D.C.: General Printing Office 1963)

would be completely achieved by federal funds whereas larger efforts in other communities would suck all the money down a black hole with few results.[57] The campaign against blight reached dramatic proportions, occupying large amounts of space in *Edgewater-Uptown News*. Letters to the editor reflected the fears of residents about the impending neighborhood decline. The lack of federal aid and inability to generate more local funding from Uptown residents frustrated some UCC members. One of the most vocal groups within the UCC was the Hazel-Hutchinson Block Group. This small enclave just east of Clarendon Avenue in the south east side of Uptown (census tract 314) boasted some of the highest property values in the city of Chicago. Some of the historic homes were designed by Louis Sullivan and Frank Lloyd Wright. In a letter addressed to families of the block, Attorney Morris Bromberg stated that, "blight and deterioration have been moving swiftly toward us."[58]

Behind this drive to conserve deteriorating neighborhoods was the widening rift between the more affluent residents of Uptown and a burgeoning population of urban newcomers. It is no mystery why the group leading the fight against the "disease" creeping toward them was adjacent to the largest concentration of southerners in Uptown.[59] With no buffer other than their tall wrought iron fences, the Hazel-Hutchenson neighborhood was sandwiched between Lake Michigan and the southern migrants. The newcomers' need for cheap housing was at odds with those of the long-time residents. Southern migrants sought inexpensive places to live in close proximity to work. Long time residents and business leaders sought increased property values, and a retail boost. Southerners would realize that moving to Chicago involved coming to grips with these opposing interests. In the eyes of many they were unwelcome newcomers. Confronting this opposition would solidify the bond of unity created by their close proximity to one another and common southern background.

Notes

1. "Uptown was Only a Subdivision 37 Years Ago," *Uptown News*, 6 February 1931.
2. A. L. T. Hoffman of the Uptown Chamber of Commerce speaking at a meeting in 1963. Minutes to a meeting on the opening of the Chicago Southern Center. Southern Appalachian Archives. (Box 284-3) Hutchinson Library, Berea College.
3. Personal interview by the author with Sergeant Bob Johnson, Chicago Police Department, 14 February 1994.
4. There are numerous historical examples involving immigrant group in cities such as, Irish and Italian immigrants in the Five Points section of New York City and San Francisco's Chinatown. Contemporary immigrants from Asian and Latin America and minorities in deteriorating inner cities are often associated with urban decay and social problems.
5. Homer Hoyt, *One Hundred Years of Land Values in Chicago* (Chicago: University of Chicago Press, 1923), 56.
6. John Drury. "Buena Park" *Learner Booster*, 13 July 1949.

7. Kenneth T. Jackson, *Crabgrass Frontier: The Suburbanization of the United States* (New York: Oxford University Press, 1985). See also Robert Fishman, *Bourgeois Utopias: The Rise and Fall of Suburbia* (New York: Basic Books, 1987).

8. <http://www.poemhunter.com/bestpoems/eugenefield/> (December 31, 2006).

9. "Elevated Stop Created Uptown Business Area." *Uptown News*, 8 July 1957.

10. "Uptown was only a Subdivision 37 Years Ago." *Uptown News*, 6 February 1931.

11. Philip Highest and Hoes Hiss, eds., *Local Community Fact Book, 1949* (Chicago: University of Chicago, 1953).

12. "Recollections" in Vivian Palmer, ed. *History of the Uptown Community of Chicago*, (Chicago: Chicago Historical Society and Local Community Research Committee, 1930).

13. James Leslie Davis, *The Elevated System and the Growth of Northern Chicago*, Evanston, Illinois: Northwestern University Department of Geography (undated), 85–103.

14. *Chicago Daily News* (undated transcribed article) Chicago Historical Society.

15. *Uptown News*, 6 February 1931 (Sultzer Regional Library news clippings).

16. <http://chicago.urban-history.org/sites/d_stores/l_miller.htm/> (December 30, 2006).

17. "Great White Way Debut Monday." *Uptown News*, 17 August 1948. "White Way to be Inaugurated Here Tomorrow," *Uptown News*, 23 August 1948, 1(N).

18. "Private Funds are Key to the Future," *Chicago Tribune*, 17 May 1962.

19. Patrick McCormick, "Fun Times in Uptown's Heyday," *Edgewater-Uptown News*, 10 February 1981, 2(N).

20. Northwestern Elevated Railroad, *Where and How to Go*, (Chicago: Northwestern Elevated Railroad, 1908).

21. Chicago Recreation Commission and Northwestern University. *The Chicago Recreation Survey, 1937* (Chicago: Chicago Recreation Commission and Northwestern University, 1930), 38.

22. <http://chicago.urban-history.org/ven/dhs/arcadia.shtml> (December 21, 2006).

23. "Fun Times in Uptown's Heyday."

24. Nancy Banks, "The World's Most Beautiful Ballrooms," *Chicago History*, Vol. 2, No.4, 1970, 206.

25. <http://chicago.urban-history.org/sites/ballroom/aragon.htm/>(December 30, 2006)

26. Lesley Sussman, "A Trip Through the Other Side of Uptown" *Edgewater Uptown News*. (undated). Sulzer Regional Library, Chicago.

27. Walter C. Reckless, *Vice in Chicago*, (Chicago: University of Chicago Press, 1933).

28. "Population Facts for Planning Chicago," Chicago: The Chicago Plan Commission, 1942.

29. "Land Use in Chicago." Prepared by the Works Progress Administration, Under the Direction of the Chicago Plan Commission, 1939.

30. Ernest Burgess and Charles Newcomb, *Census Data for Chicago, 1930* (Chicago: University of Chicago Press, 1933), 569.

31. Charles Newcomb and Richard O. Lang, *Census Data for the City of Chicago, 1934*, (Chicago: University of Chicago Press 1934), 6.

32. *Seventeenth Census of the United States, 1950*, "Characteristics of the Population by Census Tracts: 1950," (Table 2). *Eighteenth Census of the United States* "Labor Force Characteristics by Census Tracts, 1960," (Table P-3).

33. Data taken from the 1950 and the 1960 editions of the *Local Community Fact Book*, (Chicago: University of Chicago Press, 1953 and 1963).

34. Kenneth T. Jackson. *Crabgrass Frontier*, 283–285.

35. This reflects 1950 values in constant (1960) dollars. Computed with the Consumer Price Index for 1950 and 1960.

36. "Council Gets and Anti-Slum Bill," *Uptown News*, 15 May 1951, 1(N).

37. "Fire Spurs Anti-Slum Drive," *Uptown News*, 12, June 1951, 1(N).

38."Demand Action on Conversions," *Uptown News*, 3 July 1951, 1(N).

39."Private Funds Are Key to Future," *Chicago Tribune*, 17 May 1962.

40.   Jon C. Teaford. *Rough Road to Renaissance: Urban Revitalization in America, 1940–1985*. (Baltimore: Johns Hopkins University Press, 1990), 129–131.

41. David Halberstam. *The Fifties.* (New York: Fawcett, 1993), 173–178.

42. < http://www.chipublib.org/004chicago/mayors/speeches/kennelly47.html> (December 29, 2006).

43. "Men Versus Machine in Chicago," *Time*, 7 March 1955.

44. Jon C. Teaford, *The Rough Road to Renaissance*.

45. "Pick Dobbeck as Uptown President," *Edgewater-Uptown News, 5* June 1956, 1(N).

46. Uptown Chicago Commission, "Uptown Conservation Proposal," August 30, 1957, 1(N).

47. "Ask Action to Halt Slum Formation." *Edgewater Uptown News,* 18 November 1952, 1(N) .

48. "Uptown Commission Strives for $25,000 and 1000 New Members," *Edgewater-Uptown News,* 2 February 1957, 1(N).

49. "Two Uptown Landlords Charged by City Anti-Blight Campaign," *Edgewater-Uptown News,* 13 May 1957, 1(N).

50. "Bulging Buildings Bring $8000 fines." *Edgewater Uptown News*, 21 May, 1957.

51. "City Seeks to Shut Alleged 'Firetrap' Run by Two Pols," *Edgewater Uptown News*, 11 November 1957, 1(N).

52. "Uptown Turning Rooming Houses Back to Flats," *Uptown Edgewater News*, 17, December 1967, 3(N). Data for substandard housing taken from the 1950 and 1960 Censuses of the United States. "Characteristics of the Dwelling Units by Census Tracts," (Table 3).

53. Interviews with a former building manager confirmed this practice.

54. George Shibner, "Report Urges Test Plan in Uptown Area," *Chicago Tribune*, 21 December 1958.

55. "Uptown Asks $3 Million for Area Conservation," *Edgewater-Uptown News*, 1 October 1957, 1(N).

56. "Uptown Area Face-Lifting Plan Disclosed," *Chicago Daily News.* 28 September 1957.

57. "Demand North Side Get fair Share of Blight Funds." *Edgewater-Uptown News*, 16 April 1957.

58. "Hazel-Hutchenson Block Group Opens Blight Fight," *Edgewater-Uptown News,* 12 February 1957, 1(N).

59. Census data revealed that the tract immediately west of this neighborhood contained the largest percentage of migrants from the South in 1960.

Chapter 3

A Common Ground:
Urban Adaptation and Migrant Identity

Chicago was the first place I saw blacks and whites together—black men and white women or whatever. I had never seen that in my life.[1]

I was the only boy scout wearing work boots.[2]

Sarah Dotson and Donald Powell arrived in Uptown with thousands of newcomers from the South. Although there were small numbers of white southerners in Uptown as early as the 1940s, their number in no way resembled the massive influx which began in the 1950s. In the midst of the concerted efforts by the UCC, building owners, and city inspectors to ameliorate the housing in Uptown, southern migrants complicated the housing problems. Some of the qualities that attract any group of migrants to an area were targeted for eradication by others. The affordable rent, furnished apartments, transient hotels, and proximity to expanding industry in places like Skokie and Evanston were among the reasons Uptown became a port of entry. Some had no intention of remaining in Chicago for any length of time and brought no furniture. Therefore, furnished rooms appealed to some newcomers like Donald Powell. Migrants with families like Sarah Dotson sought larger more permanent arrangements. At a time when the anti-blight campaign was in full swing some southern migrants created a demand for the exact types of housing that made Uptown undesirable to many older affluent residents and business. The sudden influx of so many people created a demand that exceeded the availability of housing. As expected the newly-arrived stayed with their kinfolk or friends. Apartments were overcrowded, building facilities were strained, and parking problems were aggravated.

Many southerners came for work, opportunity, and survival, others came for more personal reasons. They were not visitors coming to Chicago to visit the historical Water Tower or the Drake Hotel. While many may have passed the Drake on their way north to Uptown, most would never even make it to the lobby of the historical hotel that Zorbaugh had written about in *The Gold Coast and the Slum*. These southerners would find Uptown more like "The World of Furnished Rooms" Zorbaugh had described in Chapter 4 of his 1929 classic.[3] Once in Uptown they found themselves in close geographic proximity to one another confronting similar challenges while adapting to urban life. All migrants had common experiences with race, employment, climate, and the rapid pace of city life. Migration left an indelible mark on those who came to Chicago, separating them from their friends and kinfolk back home. The experiences that they shared in Chicago made them more similar to each other than those they left at home in the South. In someways, they were acquiring a distinctive southern identity forged by these common experiences. Arriving in Chicago while Jim Crow flourished in the South, some had never been in the workplace or on relative equal social footing with African Americans or other races. Being white in the South, carried social status unparalleled in the North. Southern whites lost a certain amount of status after coming to Chicago. They experienced this in various ways such as an integrated workplace.

Clearly pinpointing the influx of white southerners in Uptown is not without problems.[4] With that said, certain data elucidate overall concentrations of southern migrants. Thus it is possible to identify those residents in Uptown who indicate their birthplace as being in the South. There were large numbers of African Americans in Chicago from the South but few in Uptown. During the 1950s and 1960s Uptown remained almost exclusively white which eliminated any conflation with the ongoing African American migration from the South to Chicago.[5] The height of the southern white migration to Uptown occurred probably between 1950 and 1970. By and large, the destination and concentration of southerners varied only slightly during this time. This suggests the strong influence of friends and kin on destination and settlement. Observers commenting on the migration at the time often pointed out the prevalence of licence plates from the South parked on the streets and alleys of Uptown. Southern migrants were 10 percent of all those reporting a different residence in 1955, and 5 percent of all those reporting a different residence in 1965. Despite this small drop, southern whites made up large proportions of in-migrants to certain census tracts.

In 1960, just over 4,600 people in Uptown lived in the South before coming to Chicago, roughly 17 percent of the total population. By 1970, it was under 4 percent, a 44 percent decline. However, because the census only counted those who arrived in the five previous years, there is no way of defining the exact southern population in Uptown. The Chicago Southern Center's estimates ranged from 25 to 30,000 or over 40 percent of the population in Uptown. This may be inflated but is a more reliable estimate since they had daily and ongoing contact with the southern migrant population. One way to better examine the presence of southern whites in Uptown is by examining which census tracts migrants were living. This is a rough measure of clustering. Maps 3.1 and 3.2 show the census tracts in Uptown to which southerners migrated. By 1960, 70 percent of the southern white in-migrants were concentrated in four contiguous census tracts (315, 316, 317 and 321) in 1960. Migrants continued to come to these same sub areas in Uptown. By 1970 these four census tracts attracted 71 percent of the total in-migrants from the South.[6] Assuming

Map 3.1
Percentage of Migrants from the South
to Uptown by Census Tract, 1960

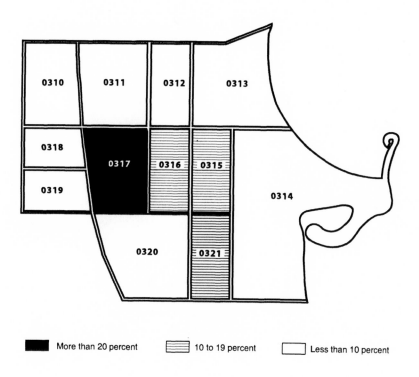

 More than 20 percent   10 to 19 percent   Less than 10 percent

Source: U.S. Bureau of the Census, Eighteenth Census of the United States. "General
Characteristics of the Population by Census Tracts, 1960" (Washington, D.C.: General
Printing Office 1963)

Map 3.2
Percentage of Migrants from the South
to Uptown by Census Tract, 1970

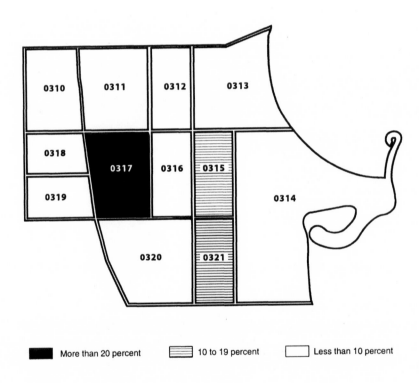

Source: U.S. Bureau of the Census, Nineteenth Census of the United States. "Social
Characteristics of the Population by Census Tracts, 1970" (Washington, D.C.: General
Printing Office 1973)

that most southern migrants who came to Uptown were remaining at least five years, their neighborhoods may have become more concentrated over time.

Local surveys are an indispensable source for precise indications of the state of origin of migrants to Uptown.[7] The Chicago Commission on Human Relations surveyed fifty-three southern whites for a neighborhood study in 1957.[8] Although small, the sample offers a snapshot of the southern states from which migrants originated (Figure 3.1). Although the southern families originated in ten southern states, a sizable majority came from Alabama, Kentucky, Tennessee and West Virginia. During the 1950s mechanization in mining displaced thousands of families in coal producing areas of these states. Their heavy presence in Uptown was probably indicative of the economic conditions in the Appalachian South.

Figure 3.2 was compiled from a sample of 1,138 southern children living in Uptown in 1963.[9] Migrants continued to represent the states of West Virginia, and Kentucky. However, Tennessee is conspicuously absent. Several things may explain this. First, this sample was much larger and therefore may be a much more accurate representation. Second, previous research found Tennesseans primarily on the west side of Chicago rather than in Uptown which is on the north side.[10] In 1963, over 80 percent of the migrants in Uptown were from mountain counties. The predominance of mountaineers reflect the changes in the technology of mining that displaced large numbers of miners from work.

The most prevalent image of the people of Chicago for Americans may have been shaped by Stud Turkel's oral histories of its residents. His attention to the details that seldom make history, but remain important to those people who shape history appeal to us on a number of levels. Both his subjects and those that I interviewed remind us that the seemingly ordinary figures very prominently in memories. It is no surprise that the arrival in Chicago, a seemingly insignificant event, represented a profound event in the individual lives of white southern migrants. It is vividly etched in their minds. Virginia Bowers was no exception to others who were able to recall the weather, details of conversations on a day they may have experienced thirty years in the past. Similar to the black southerners arriving in Chicago that James Gregory chronicled in *Land of Hope*, southern whites needed no help deciding where to go once they got to Chicago. Much like Harlem, Uptown loomed large in the minds of white southerners. Moreover much like black southerners arriving in New York, most assumed that all white southerners "belonged" in Uptown. For those who came by bus or automobile, the road trip took them past the steel mills on the south side, past the Loop with its magnificent high rises, past the affluent Gold Coast, to Uptown.

It is difficult to paint a typical picture of arrival. Virginia Bowers arrived on a Greyhound bus and was taken on a tour of skid row, Helen Elam arrived on the train, Donald Powell and James Lambert drove into Chicago. From one account in *Mountain Life and Work* a typical first day in Uptown began with a family waking up inside their car which they parked in front of a relative's apartment building. The parents were 35 to 40 years old with eighth-grade educations. Once awake, the wife departed with the kids to locate the friend or relative to rent an apartment, and the

48

Figure 3.1
Southern White Migrants in Uptown, 1957
State of Origin

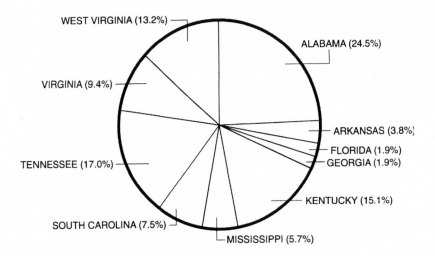

Source: Bert Schloss, "The Uptown Area and the Southern White In-Migrant," Chicago
Commissionon Human Relations, 1957.

Figure 3.2
Southern White Migrants in Uptown, 1963
State of Origin

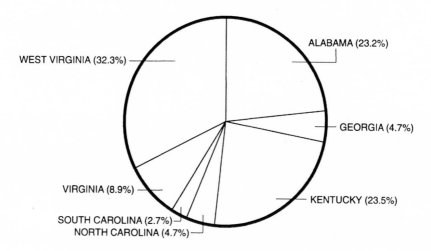

Source: Victor B. Strufert, "A Study of Adjustment in Uptown, (unpublished research proposal submitted to the Chicago Southern Center, November1963).

husband went to find a daily employment agency or sell a pint of blood.[11] Most arrived unnoticed as anyone might at a friend's or relative's apartment. The stories of arrival reveal the depth of experiences, perceptions, and feelings that each person underwent in coming to Chicago.

At fifty-one J.D. Donnelson was one of the youngest migrants that I had interviewed. His life had been a series of unstable jobs, a failed marriage, prison, and drug abuse. His mother came to Chicago after divorcing her husband. She had brothers and sisters living in Uptown on Clifton Street near Sunnyside Avenue. J.D. remembered the role his family played in his decision to come to Chicago. "I came to Chicago because my mother was here. I had about four aunts and uncles already here, and they had relatives that had migrated years ago that owned property, bars, and things. That's why we could migrate, because we had other people that we could stay with till we got jobs."[12] Kinfolk facilitated migration and urban adaptation. Friends and kin provided a certain familiarity and order to a new setting. Relatives and friends taught migrants to become streetwise, and find employment and housing. This is not unlike other immigrant groups in urban areas throughout history. Families, however, were not always centers of warmth and harmony. Although J.D.'s relatives helped him initially, he was later thrown out and turned to male prostitution for a brief period of time.

Whether people left home willingly or unwillingly they shared a sentimentality about the places they left behind. Migrants and immigrants tended to share a nostalgia about home. For some the desire to return was greater than for others. And for some the impediments are greater. Because of the loss of place, many migrants in Uptown were preoccupied with returning home or considered Chicago something temporary. Over time as children were born and roots were established in Uptown returning home became more difficult, impractical and improbable. Andrena Belcher came to Uptown from Kentucky with her parents, Bill and Clara when she was three years old. Her parents wanted employment and the opportunity to escape the mines where friends and kin had either been killed or stricken with black lung disease. She believed that Chicago would be temporary home. "We kept thinking that we were gonna come back [home]. I mean, we didn't ever go and settle in Chicago thinking that was home."[13] Her mother and sister, Belinda still live in Uptown. When I interviewed her in 1996, Helen Elam had lived in Uptown for thirty years. She stated that she "never meant to stay here in all the years, I've stayed."[14]

For some, the immediate impulse was to return to familiar surroundings. A former gang worker who had extensive contact with southern youth and their families pointed out that living in Chicago challenged other world views as well: "Being up here in the North in Uptown or anywhere in Chicago was degrading to the people. Back home the land belonged to the family. This [life in Chicago] was not what people were used to. They were confined."[15] The apartments in Chicago were smaller and, in many cases, overcrowded. Chicago was so big and difficult to escape. There was no space to get away. Children had to play under the elevated tracks amid broken bottles and trash. Men could not hunt, nor could they carry firearms as they did down home.

Settlement involved a variety of new experiences. In an early essay in urban sociology, "The Metropolis and Mental Life" Georg Simmel explored the elements that separated urban dwellers from their rural counterparts. It was Simmel's contention that the foundation of individuality would be swept up in the rapid current of urban life resulting in what he termed a blasé outlook. Part of this involved sensory bombardment that individuals experienced in cities. This is often omitted in discussions of urban migration. Although it was not Simmel's intention to discuss urban migration, he does point up an important aspect of migration involving sensory perception. Migrants had to adjust to the elevated trains, and incessant noise they produced as they rumbled past twenty feet above. The loud noise, the perplexity of its mechanical success, and sheer size impressed newcomers to the city. Helen Elam refused to ride the elevated trains for several years after arriving in Uptown. She was forced to take the bus to work in the Loop. It was only after she learned that the elevated line would be faster that she considered taking it. Even then it took some reassurance from her family to ride the train. Her comments remind us of how the seemingly mundane elements of urban living presented obstacles to adjusting to life in Chicago. "I was scared to death of the elevated subway. It took my living here three or four years for my cousins to coax me on the el." Migrants were particularly aware of the elevated trains because they were so pervasive in their neighborhood. The Howard line ran diagonally through Uptown. It literally split the community in half. To get anywhere east or west through Uptown they had to pass under the massive tracks. It scared children particularly if a train passed while walking under the tracks. In most places in Uptown today residents are reminded of the trains running eye level to the second floor of apartments. For those unable to see the trains there is the constant sound as a reminder. As in so many other cities their presence has been assimilated with the garbage trucks, sirens, and screams to which one is accustomed.

Chicago's climate has been recognized by observers for centuries. During the summer the humid heat kept people on back porches, on front stairs or wherever some breeze could be found. The winter, however was the hardest on newcomers from the South. While originally the term windy city was used to promote Chicago as a summer vacation destination, the winds of the winter are brutal, and drive down the wind chill to below zero. Blowing snow whipped around each corner during the winter like a cold slap in the face. Sometimes there were snowdrifts. Mounds of plowed snow made crossing streets difficult in the winter. Some streets like Clifton received no attention after heavy snowfalls. Snow-covered cars sat like silent tombs waiting to be uncovered or blocked in by a passing snow plow. One of the few Texans in Uptown, Loretta Adrahtas arrived in the winter of 1955. As were most migrants, she was shocked by the cold weather. Her husband intended to find work, but the harsh weather and her husband's ill heath forced him to go back home. She and her seven children remained in Uptown. "When I came up here, there was snow all the way up to the windows all the time and we weren't used to that."[16] Similarly, Donald Powell and his friends were unprepared for the change in temperature in

Chicago. The climate change impacted him severely. He remembered arriving in the
Winter from Tuscaloosa.

> We didn't know how cold it was up here. We had on short sleeve shirts, pair of
> pants and regular tennis shoes. It felt like it was fifteen below zero. Every time
> winter gets here, I remember coming to Chicago, you know, and I want to go
> straight back home. And every time Spring comes I want to go home too. And I
> do sometimes.[17]

The climate became a time marker of arrival in Chicago. Because it could be so
harsh and seemingly unrelenting, the climate forced a continual comparison of home
with Chicago. In this case weather is the comparison. The experience with a change
of climate is not unique to southerners. Italian immigrants also experienced a
dramatic climate change when they arrived in New York City in large numbers
beginning in the 1880s. Similar to southerners, Italians longed to return to Italy
when the weather moderated in the spring. It also made working outside unstable
and difficult.[18]

Even for those migrating from urban areas in the South, Chicago was a place
of dramatic contrasts in scale as well as norms. Chicago was also more
heterogeneous than the smaller towns in the South. Compared to smaller towns
where wealth is less conspicuous, class more obscured, poverty, and racial
oppression better hidden, the city appeared obsessed with the display of these
elements. Compared to the order of home, the city appeared to exist in a certain
disorder. In the South there was spatial simplicity and physical and social order in
relationships including those involving race. Many of these familiar patterns had to
be recreated in the city.

Urban adaptation also involved developing a sixth sense for urban predators.
They had to develop a street sense. Friends and relatives were indispensable in this
process. They instructed migrants about which stores were legitimate, how to
negotiate a dark street, where to carry money, and who to trust. For the first time
doors had to be locked at night or when away from home. Kinfolk often provided
important lessons about the city. In 1959, Virginia took a bus from Arkansas to
Chicago. The Greyhound got in on Memorial Day morning. Her sister and brother-
in-law who had arrived in 1958 met her at the station. They were going to let her
stay with them until she found a job and an apartment. After leaving the bus
terminal she was taken on a tour of the West Madison skid row district. Her brother-
in-law insisted on showing her this area in order to show her that certain parts of
Chicago were dangerous.

> After I got to the bus station, they took me on a tour of skid row. Skid Row!
> That's Right! All these drunks laying around on the curb, you know. You gotta be
> kiddin'. No one does this. Then, we stopped at a red light, and here comes this guy
> down a flight of stairs on the outside of a bar and rooms up over it. And you could
> just barely hear him: 'help me, help me' and blood just a pouring. I started across
> the street to help, and they said 'come back here, come back here, you don't get

involved in nothin' like this' I said 'what do you mean you don't get
involved?' They said, 'huh uh, no.' It didn't take me long to get used to it.[19]

This reflects a central theme involved in migration: being introduced to an
urban lifestyle involving a passive disinterest in events for self preservation
purposes. The quotation above illustrates the process of becoming streetwise.
This process involved developing a set of informal rules and behavior for use
in public space. This street wisdom allowed southerners safe passage while
avoiding trouble and conflict. Andrena Belcher recalled her father telling her
as a little girl in Uptown "to walk on the outside of the sidewalk near the curb
and run into the street if there was trouble." Elijah Anderson argued that "street
wisdom is a way of negotiating day-to-day actions with minimum risk and
maximum mutual respect in a world full of uncertainty and danger."[20]
Southerners created an ambivalence toward their surroundings while
simultaneously surveying other pedestrians and events. Although this process
is said to emerge through trial and error, the cases of Andrena and Virginia
illustrated the importance of kinfolk in this process. Their kin became the street
guides who familiarized them with the city and its danger. The shock of seeing
a bloody man, was as fixed in Virginia's memory of arrival as was the climate
was for Donald Powell.

Perhaps the most obvious change upon arrival was the racial order of
Chicago. While many black southerners conceived of Chicago as a "land of
hope" in socio-political terms compared to the South, white southerners were
unprepared for the improved social status minorities enjoyed in Chicago. White
southerners had come to Chicago from a climate of racial oppression in the
South. It may be interesting to recall that the Emit Till lynching became
national news during the height of the white southern migration to Chicago.
Some relatives of migrants interviewed were racist while others had been
members of the Ku Klux Klan back home. People knew what it meant to be
white and black in the South, however, southern segregation shielded whites
from the raw effects of oppression. While race relations in Chicago were not
harmonious, racial etiquette was different and, races came into closer personal
contact on more equal footing that in the South. Newcomers came into contact
with members of other racial and ethnic groups on public transit, at work, on
the street, and in stores. This left a lasting impression on Virginia Bowers:

> Chicago was the first place I saw blacks and whites together. Black men and white
> women or whatever, you know. I had never seen that before in my life, you know.
> No one did that back home. I'd see blacks going in restaurants with whites or
> alone if they wanted. Back home they couldn't do that. Before I got to Chicago I
> just thought that was the way it was, you know. I didn't know what prejudice
> was.[21]

The experience of seeing different races socializing caused some pause and reflection. When in a tavern, migrants were struck by the degree to which the races interacted on a much more casual and intimate level than they were allowed to back home. Migrants were surprised at this different form of social interaction:

> I remember going out to this place on Lawrence and seeing blacks and whites out together. Everybody dancing, blacks and whites, everybody getting along good, having a good time. No fights or nothing. I said [to myself] man you wouldn't find that down south. you wouldn't find that in my home town. Everybody was white.[22]

While women tended to accept the greater degree of racial interaction, men often rebelled. Blacks and whites rubbed elbows so to speak more in Chicago than in the South. This closer proximity meant more intense measures taken to enforce southern racial norms in the neighborhood. Store keepers kept "bats reserved for niggers," men formed groups to regulate blacks similar to the Ku Klux Klan and resented even the small presence of African Americans in Uptown. An unofficial boundary line existed near Leland and Winthrop. If blacks were seen crossing the divide they would be beaten or threatened with death. One long time black resident recalled not being able to go to the corner drug store because it was on the white side of the street.[23] He went on to say that blacks in Uptown did not want to understand or trust southern whites. Although blacks in Uptown did not overtly seek integration, they expected legal and political protections under the law. There was no guarantee, however, that white southerners would always comply. It seemed on some occasions that Jim Crow was transplanted to Uptown. Well into the 1960s, Uptown bars still denied blacks service. A bartender at Whitey's bar on Kenmore Avenue was arrested for refusing to serve two black city workers. After being ignored, and then told that the cooler was broken, the bartender finally told them that he wouldn't serve them because they were black.[24]

Southerners were unprepared for the effect their arrival was having on other Chicagoans. Given the widespread hillbilly stereotypes in Chicago, southerners experienced prejudice first hand albeit mildly. While not comparable to the prejudice that blacks experienced southern whites found Chicago somewhat less hospitable than they imagined. Earlier when Lewis Killian studied southern whites in Chicago he found them unwelcome in taverns in the 1940s.[25] Previous studies of southern whites in Detroit and Chicago found that southerners experienced a loss of social status after coming to northern cities. Many reacted to this by becoming staunch supporters of the southern racial order and proud of their heritage.

> In Chicago they [southern whites] found themselves only one group in a mosaic of diverse ethnic groups. The fact that they were white native born and Protestant lost some of its prestige value. Negroes while subject to many subtle forms of discrimination in Chicago possessed far more freedom and power than they could enjoy in the South.[26]

While not leading to formal organizations, this loss of status often led southern migrants to reestablish the racial order by voluntary segregation in taverns, praising southern racial segregation, and reacting to violations of southern social norms. As mentioned, some tried to transplant southern racial norms to Chicago. Whether this was an attempt to regain the loss of status or not is unknown. Intra-race relations were not without conflict. Southern whites who overtly crossed the racial divide were dealt with harshly by those who clung to racial views brought from the South. In some cases violence was used to intimidate transgressors. Virginia recalled an incident involving a racist building manager from Tennessee. Virginia became involved in the struggle for civil rights. She was active in an SDS program, JOIN (Jobs or Income Now). This brought her into contact with African Americans. She also worked with blacks in Chicago. In one incident the building manager was upset because she invited African Americans to her apartment.

> When I moved into this apartment on Sunnyside, the manager was from Tennessee, very racist. He couldn't stand it because me and my two black friends were always going out together. We worked together. He really . . . he really got to be something else. So we met with some black groups, and went to his door. He wouldn't come. He sent his wife to the door. [27]

The situation escalated into a confrontation with the manager. Virginia allied herself with the members of the Black Panthers and a Chicago street gang. After an initial altercation with the manager he retaliated by dropping bricks from an upper floor of the building onto her friend's car. He then saw that her lease was not renewed. Similarly, when two African Americans spent the night on Virginia's couch neighbors intimidated her by throwing fire works into a narrow hallway damaging her young son's hearing. Such events point out the tension involved in race relations and the limitation of legal protections in addressing conflict. Moreover, acceptance of new racial norms caused family rifts, affected the frequency of visits back home, and the intimacy of the relationship with her family members declined.

> I lost closeness with my family because they were so prejudice. I am the only one [in my family] that has black friends, or Spanish friends. I'd go home and listen to this nigger, nigger, you know. Then I'd come back to Chicago and just go about my business. When I do go home, I just keep my mouth shut.[28]

More importantly, it demonstrated how individual convictions sometimes took precedence over family. In this case, Virginia's experience upon arrival had lasting implications in her decision to turn to community organizing. Her convictions also negatively impacted relations with family members. Her brother disowned her for participating in the Civil Rights Movement.

Although less than one percent of the population of Uptown until 1980, African Americans were not the only minority group that southern migrants encountered. Being in the North also meant contact with Latinos. This provoked a reaction about the uses of English in places like the factory. Southerners found that some Puerto Ricans, Mexicans, and Cubans spoke Spanish to communicate to coworkers at the

Continental Can Company. Southern migrants found this irritating and offensive. In one case, Sarah Dotson became annoyed at the two Cuban coworkers when they used Spanish at work. There was an implicit pride and sense of insult in her remarks about her experience:

> I didn't know that people talked Spanish in Chicago. I didn't know what to think about that. The second job I got, it was a lot of Cuban girls. And they were talking Spanish. So I told them. I wish you'd talk something that I could understand. I don't know if you're talking about me, or what. You're over here making our money. Why don't you speak our English. Then I rubbed my finger together like this [indicated money] and said, you understand this, don't you?[29]

Although there is a distinct tinge of xenophobia in Sarah's comments, they point to the animosity engendered in the workplace when newcomers compete economically with each other. When migrants first arrived they also experienced ethnic conflict with older German immigrants. Sarah Dotson's family encountered unfriendly neighbors when they moved to Uptown. "When we came, Germans from the old country hated us 'cause we were from the hills. [They'd always tell us] 'Go back to where you come from. Go back to where you come from.' They'd always get onto my boys." Contact with other ethnic groups sometimes led to violent confrontations. Donald Powell related an event in 1964 in which southern whites had to fight Puerto Ricans for the right to use and inhabit a street. "We had to fight for Clifton Avenue. We had to take Clifton Avenue from the Puerto Ricans to live there." This ended when two leaders of the rival groups fought and one knocked the other out. Following this, according to Donald, "The Puerto Ricans started moving out."[30] Killian also found similar conflict between Italian Americans and southern whites in the Near North Side of Chicago in the 1940s.[31]

By and large the legal status accorded to African Americans and other immigrants forced southerners to reevaluate their southern style racism. While there was no Jim Crow in Chicago racist attitudes tended to persist among men. Men tended to cling to ideas of racial superiority. Women, however, frequently reacted differently after being exposed to social situations involving inter-racial contact. Virginia reevaluated her opinions about racial superiority and oppression. This had profound implications for her future in Uptown, her racial attitudes, and when she returned to visit her relatives in Arkansas. After experiencing the racial norms in Chicago, she reacted strongly to the strict segregation and social treatment of African Americans back home. Her responses, however, conflicted with those of her family and friends still living in the South. At times her behavior provoked a response from others around her. Virginia would not retreat from her principles when it came to racial prejudice. While more dangerous in the South, she never hesitated to come to the defense of blacks even when it violated racial etiquette.

> When I came to Chicago, and then would go back South and see how the blacks were treated. I mean, I would get up in a restaurant and I would get myself up to go and help

the black person. And I'd have to be drug back down and they'd [people she was with] say, 'look you're not in Chicago. We don't do that.' When I'd go back I'd see how hard it was [for blacks] you know?[32]

Similar sentiments were recorded by earlier works of Southern whites in Chicago. When discussing this issue southern migrants in Chicago alluded to a change in racial attitudes in specific situations, such as restaurants, after living in Chicago. While not as active of a reaction, the perception reflects new attitudes about race. "You know, the last time I was in Tennessee I went to a restaurant. They served colored but they made 'em go in the back door and eat in the kitchen. I told my husband, that it looked funny after you've lived in Chicago" [33] Clearly, an alteration in her normative reference for social behavior took place. Segregation once may have appeared natural to southern whites but now often appeared awkward and socially askew.

Although somewhat different, previous evidence indicated a complete change in attitudes concerning interracial dating, for example. Men rarely expressed comfort with this topic. Women, who had been socialized against people of color, behaved differently once in Chicago. One of the women in Gitlin and Hollander's work *Uptown* discussed the effect living in Chicago had on her views, and patterns of interracial dating. Linda, who was twenty-one at the time of the interview had the following remark about race and dating. Linda recalled being, "taught to hate colored people. I was taught to kill one if they ever asked me for a date. Since I been up here I dated more colored boys than I can count."[34] This is more important because it represented a fundamental shift in behavior and participation in public. It was important that when comparisons were made between the South and Chicago their point of reference had begun to change. This not only affected perceptions of race relations in the South, this demonstrated more generally how migration separated a person from the South socially. It is perhaps less of a function of being from the South than being exposed to others, or being confronted with the issue personally that loosens opposition to intermarriage. Helen Elam pointed out that is was when a member of her family became involved that her views changed. When I interviewed her, she expressed pride in her family racial diversity: "We've integrated. Some of us have married blacks. One cousin brought a girl home from Singapore, another from Turkey. It's different when you say something about other people than when your daughter comes home with someone. So we're an integrated family."[35] This is perhaps more important for Helen because of the legacy of racism among her family members, especially males in the South. As seen, accepting racial diversity was sometimes matter of choosing sides, which had repercussions for friends and family.

Southerners also had to adjust to a drastic reduction in size of their new accommodations. Most migrants lived in cramped one or two-bedroom apartments; many of which were furnished, which was standard in many buildings at the time. Most were accustomed to more space both inside and outside. When Ruby Hanks came to Chicago in 1957 she and her two sons lived in a one-room apartment. After

her husband arrived, they moved into a two-room apartment in the same building
with a small kitchen. In Ruby's case, this meant a drastic reduction in space. She
and her husband had lived in a house with a great deal of adjoining land in West
Virginia. Donald Powell and Brenda Scraggs moved into a furnished one-bedroom
apartment with their daughter in 1967. Sometimes, a family of four lived in two
rooms with a sofa bed in one room, and a pull down bed in another room.

Women often had to make the largest adjustments by adding responsibilities
rather than shedding them. The arrangement in which women work a second shift
of housework is common among couples who both work outside the home. Most
families arranged the house and child care by juggling schedules at work. In order
to care for their children Ruby and her husband worked different shifts. However,
there was still the ongoing work of cleaning, cooking, washing, and ironing for her
husband and children. According to Ruby, this was what had most changed in her
life.

> You had twice the work to do. You had to do your job [in the factory] and you had
> to come in and do the housework, and you had to do your laundry. Back then you
> ironed everything that you dried. and you cooked stuff for dinner for the old man
> and kids.[36]

This type of schedule dramatically affected the pace and routine in which tasks were
accomplished in the house. There was a clear tradeoff. Chores that had been
performed back home such as lighting a coal stove for warmth and cooking were
replaced by the light industrial employment. Although a switch could heat the
house, the trade off was less time in the home, and less time together with her
husband and children. Randy and Linda Hamilton worked different shifts and
utilized a baby sitter very efficiently. When interviewed in their living room in
Uptown Randy summed up the accommodation that took place: "Hell, I worked
second-shift at a steel plant in Evanston and Linda worked first shift somewhere so
we only had a couple of hours that we needed a sitter for the kids. I'd leave for work
around two thirty and she'd get in about three thirty or so."[37] In their case the baby
sitter was a member of their extended family who lived on the same street. Families
devised creative means to cover for each other including leaving their children with
neighbors.

Many southern white women managed buildings in which other southerners
lived. Some women and actually managed two buildings simultaneously. Typically,
managers lived in apartments in the building in return for reduction or waiver of
rent. Building managers were the eyes and ears of the neighborhood. There were
more practical advantages to being a manager: women could stay home with young
children; managers had first pick of the newer furniture in vacant apartments; and
access to the basement and often a garage. This gave shade tree mechanics, like Bill
Belcher, the ability earn extra money.

Landlords wanted southerners to manage buildings with southern tenants. It
was a way to remain aloof from the often dirty business of collecting rent and

dealing with tenant complaints. For their part managers were the gatekeepers who discouraged unwanted tenants from moving into the building, and protected southerners from the housing discrimination that was so pervasive during the time. Managers could bypass formal requirements and overlook inadequate conditions. Donald Powell benefitted from this when he rented his first apartment in Uptown at age seventeen. His first apartment was on Lawrence and Malden Avenues. A woman from his hometown who knew his mother allowed he and his friend to rent an apartment in spite of the fact that they were underage.[38] In this case, having a common connection to home facilitated easy entrance to his first apartment in Uptown. Because she knew his mother, the manager knew that Donald was less likely to skip out without paying the rent.

One negative aspect of being a manager for a southern migrant was presiding over buildings in substandard condition. Because so many of the buildings in Uptown were in poor condition, managers often faced the stress of complaints from tenants. If the building was in need of repair or violated municipal codes, managers were often forced to cover up for appalling or dangerous conditions. Some managers were instructed as to how to deceive inspectors investigating reports of rats and other municipal housing code violations. For Virginia Bowers being a manager was the catalyst in her decision to enter into community organizing after refusing to deceive the housing inspectors.

> I lost my first manager's job over on Kenmore because I stood up for one couple in a building where their baby had been bitten by a rat. And the owner wanted me to lie to the inspector and say that one apartment that he had fixed up was like all the others in the building. Finally, I told Tom [the inspector] I couldn't lie to him anymore, because I was a mother myself.[39]

A sense of fairness and southern unity overrode the concern for her position. She could not, in good conscience, perpetuate conditions that harmed others and would eventually lead to her being mistrusted by other southerners. Not all managers were as inclined to surrender their place of residence for their convictions. Women like Charlotte who may not have given up her apartment and manager's position for such a cause. She had five children to support and lived with her husband in a four-room apartment. The manager position allowed them to make ends meet.[40]

There is a paucity of official data on labor force participation of southern whites in Uptown because they are invisible in social statistics like the census. When I interviewed migrants about their work experience and employment history, most had favorable impressions. They claimed that there was an over abundance of work in Chicago, and that it was not difficult to locate employment. Several people that I interviewed claimed that you could quit one job and be employed the same day.[41] Some official data was collected by the Cook County Department of Public Aid.[42] Interviews yielded a more complete occupational picture. To support their families, southern men worked in every conceivable job. At Companies like Bell and Howell in Skokie, southern men and women assembled thousands of Polaroid cameras. Both Continental Can and LaSalle Candy companies in Chicago employed many southern women. It is particular interesting to hear women discuss their experiences with work in Chicago. Most had never worked outside the home before coming to Uptown. Helen Elam discussed the experience of southern women working in Chicago.

> Most of the women I knew worked. Like my mother and two of my aunts all worked at LaSalle Candies. Women worked at different factories like Continental Can. There were sewing machine factories. My aunt found a job two weeks after she got up here at LaSalle Candies as a packer. Fifty dollars a week, she made.[43]

When Sarah Dotson arrived in 1959, she intended to work outside the home. She had come to Chicago on a bus with her children thinking that he husband, Thurman, would be in Chicago. As it turns out he did not intend to remain and had taken a bus back to Williamson, West Virginia thinking that Sarah would return when she saw that he went back home. Sarah had no intention of going back to West Virginia. After enrolling her two young children in school, her husband's cousin helped her get a job the day after arriving in Uptown. She described the process as follows:

> My cousin set over for me what really is his [her husband Thurman] cousin. That evening she found out that I was in town. I went over by her house and she said 'you wanna go to work? I said, 'yeah I wanna go to work.' She said, 'go out with me in the morning and you can get a job I can get you a job where I'm at.' [Letric Metals in Skokie] So I went and got the kids and went over to her house that night. Got up the next morning and went out with her and went to work that day. And the old man [her husband Thurman] was down there [West Virginia]. He had just bought a brand new electric lawnmower, and he sold it to her brother-in-law. He seen that I was not coming back . And he sold the lawn mover to his brother-in-law with a bunch of tools, and come back up here.[44]

Most of those interviewed believed that work was plentiful in Chicago. Southern men worked at Zenith assembling color televisions. In Morton Grove H.M. Harper Steel and Warwick manufacturing employed migrants. Migrants also worked at the Teletype Corporation and Ditto incorporated. Combined Insurance employed southern men and women in several areas. Typically men were employed in maintenance and women in punch card operations.[45] Helen Elam stated that people were willing to work in any occupation. "The men worked in machine shops, they worked as truck drivers, they worked as cooks, they even worked as dishwashers. I knew that they worked at Temple Steel, Haydot Casting Company, and Continental Can."[46] By the time Donald Powell arrived in 1963, former governor Marlin of West Virginia had migrated to Uptown and was driving a cab for the Flash Cab Company.[47] He was eager to work, and found a job in Bell and Howell assembling cameras. Although too young to be employed according to company policy, a friend from Tuscaloosa made sure this did not prohibit him from getting the position.[48] This was common according to others. The dynamic of social networks operating in southern neighborhoods resulted in many southern migrants working in the same place. Employers knew that if they employed a southerner there would soon be more asking for work. There was often a primary tie such as a common county in the South, family or friendship. An employer in Chicago described in an almost comical way how southerners formed occupational groups based on a kinship or geography by claiming that, "somebody from Tennessee must have put a cross on our door. Southerners have just streamed in here looking for work, and most of them seemed to come from the same community in Tennessee. A lot of them were related to each other."[49]

Most southerners considered Chicago a good place to find work. Few migrants reported trouble finding employment. This is reflected in some official accounts of the time. In 1957, fifty-three southern white families were interviewed in Uptown about their experiences locating employment in Chicago. Of those, only five had difficulty locating work in Chicago. In some families both parents were employed. In the majority of the families interviewed, however, only one family member worked outside the home. While somewhat different from the accounts of both spouses working, there may be a number of reasons for this. Building management was probably not considered official employment by migrants or those conducting the survey. Because women were more likely work as building managers, it may have appeared that only one member of the family was officially employed. In the same survey southerners were asked about their job satisfaction. Most southerners interviewed were content with their employment. Only two men and one woman indicated that they were dissatisfied with their positions.[50]

Employers, however, had mixed impressions of southern whites. Some employers were not as satisfied with their job performances as the southerners were with their positions. Some employers considered them undependable. Moreover some employers judged southern women to be better employees than southern men. In many cases, women acquired a better reputation as workers than men. The tendency for males to return home, and the women to remain in Chicago earned women a better reputation among employers. An observer in the 1960s commented on the propensity of men to be regarded as a risk for employers and the reasons behind this.

> I think the fact that the man is an unskilled laborer doesn't command the same respect in the family as his wife does. I have talked to employers about this. The woman can be counted on to show up every day and do her job and they are good workers, but you can't say the same for the man. He is not liable to show up. He'll be down in Kentucky hunting for work.[51]

The reasons behind the reputation alluded to may be more complex than what is immediately apparent. Men may have experienced a loss of status because of the low wages, the cycle of daily pay, the instability of well-paying jobs, coupled with the independence women experienced in the city. Beneath Sarah's determination to find work and remain in Chicago, and Thurman's reluctance to come may be this differential status. Clearly Thurman did not perceive the city in the same terms as Sarah. This may account for the sporadic work habits, and frequent trips down home. These comments from employers may refer to a small group of southern men rather than all of them. Nevertheless, what does emerge from the comments is that women acquired a reputation among employers as reliable employees. Whether this reputation was accurate is not known. It certainly was a strong perception on the part of employers. In addition there were extremely negative stereotypes about southern whites that supported the comments by the employer quoted above.

During the course of settlement in Chicago, southern whites developed a common unity based on similar experiences with urban adaptation. Although the crime, the weather, the hectic pace, race relations, and new gender roles sometimes shocked and disturbed southern migrants, those factors also gave them a common identity. This identity distinguished them from family members back home. Geographic and physical separation initiated an emotional and psychological separation as well. Eventually migrants in Chicago had more in common with each other than they had with their friends and kinfolk who remained in the South. Some tried to maintain their old identity by returning to the South frequently while others willingly embraced their new life in Chicago. Much of this depended on the degree of stability they experienced in Chicago. With each marriage, or child born, or spouse buried, they strengthened their identity and connection to their community. Women developed an identity separate from their counterparts in the South. They became accustomed to working and earning their own money. They experienced more independence in Chicago. They enjoyed walking several blocks to shop in the numerous stores in Uptown. This allowed women a certain prerogative of independence which often challenged the basis of their former domestic lives in the South. Men had to come to terms with an identity that included more independence for their wives and daughters, and different racial etiquette that of the South.

Notes

1. Personal interview by the author with Virginia Bowers, 18 March 1994.
2. Personal interview by the author with Kenny Dotson, 20 June 1994.
3. Harvy Zorbaugh, *The Gold Coast and The Slum: A Sociological Study of Chicago's Near North Side* (Chicago: University of Chicago Press, 1929).
4. Official sources such as the census offer a glimpse of southern in-migration, yet mask exact numbers because of frequent return migration, and the complications of race. Southern whites are invisible to the extent that they are not identifiable by any particular surnames or ethnicity. The U.S. Census contained a question about residence in 1955 and 1965 which included "South" as a response. This data is available for the census tract level for the 1960 and 1970 censuses. Limitations with this include, no state of origin, no data on return migration, or migratory flow during the intermediary period.
5. The Chicago Fact Book Consortium, ed., Local Community Fact Book, (Chicago: University of Illinois, 1985).

6. 1960 data taken from U.S. Bureau of the Census, *Eighteenth Census of the United States*, "General Characteristics of the Population by Census Tracts, 1960" (Washington, D.C. Government Printing Office, 1960). 1970 data taken from U.S. Bureau of the Census, *Nineteenth Census of the United States*, "Social Characteristics of the Population by Census Tracts, 1970" (Washington, D.C. Government Printing Office, 1970).

7. Results must be taken with caution. Studies may have been limited to specific sub-areas, and thus one or a few states may be over represented. Southerners from the same state populated a building and in many cases, migrants from the same county group together.

8. Bert Schloss,"The Uptown Community Area and the Southern White In-Migrant." (Unpublished report, Chicago Commission on Human Relations, 1957).

9. Victor B. Strufert, "A Study of Adjustment in Uptown" (Unpublished research proposal submitted to the Chicago Southern Center, 1963).

10. L ewis Killian, Southern White Laborers in Chicago's West Side. (Unpublished Ph.D. diss., University of Chicago, 1949).

11. Bill Montgomery, "The Uptown Story" *Mountain Life and Work* (September 1968):8

12. Personal interview by the author with John "J.D." Donnelson, 19 March 1994.

13. Andrena Belcher in the film *Long Journey Home*. The Appleshop, Whitesburg, Ky., 1991.

14. Personal interview by the author with Helen Elam, 18 December 1994.

15. Personal interview by the author with Pat Milne, 17 February 1994.

16. Interview with Loretta Adrahtas in *Keep Strong*, August, 1980:39.

17. Personal interview by the author with Donald Powell, 20 June 1994.

18. Partick J. Gallo, *Old Bread New Wine: A Portrait of the Italian Americans* (Chicago: Nelson Hall, 1981), 27

19. Bowers interview

20. *Long Journey Home.*

21. Bowers interview.

22. Elam interview.

23. Personal interview by the author with Elias White, 6 April 1995.

24. "Charge Bartender With Refusing Negroes," *Edgerwater-Uptown News,* 7 July 1964, 1(N).

25. Lewis Killian,"Southern White Laborers in Chicago's West Side" (Unpublished Ph.D. diss.,University of Chicago, 1949), 318.

26. Lewis M. Killian, "The Effects of Southern White Workers on Race Relations in Northern Plants," *American Sociological Review* 17(1952) :327–331.

27. Bowers interview.

28. Bowers interview.

29. Personal interview by the author with Sarah Dotson, 8 September 1994.

30. Powell interview.

31. Killian, "Southern White Laborers," 318.

32. Bowers interview.

33. Lewis Killian, "The Adjustment of Southern White Migrants to Northern Urban Norms," *Social Forces* 32 (October 1953).

34. Todd Gitlin and Nancy Hollander, *Uptown: Poor Whites in Chicago*. New York: Harper and Row, 1970), 266–268.

35. Personal interview by the author with Helen Elam, 21 September 1994.

36. Personal interview by the author with Ruby Hanks, 8 September 1994

37. Personal interview by the author with Randy Hamilton, 8 September 1994.

38. Powell interview.

39. Bowers interview.

40. Gitlin and Hollander, *Uptown: Poor Whites in Chicago*: 241–243.

41. When a company policy forbade Sarah and her husband from working in the same company, Sarah stated that she quit and went across the street and found a job the same day. Interview, 20 June 1994.

42. "The Southern Appalachian Migrant on Public Aid in Cook County." (Unpublished report, Cook County Department of Public Aid, 1963).

43. Elam interview.

44. Personal interview by the author with Sarah Dotson, June 20, 1994.

45. In a rare example this was discussed in a letter dated March 22, 1966 to *Reader's Digest* from William Meyers, Director of Public Relations and Advertising at Combined Insurance. Southern Appalachian Archives (Box 289-9).

46. Elam interview.

47. Mentioned in the minutes of the Chicago Southern Center on March 19, 1965. Subsequently confirmed with the Flash Cab Company in Chicago, October 1994.

48. Personal interview by the author with Donald Powell, June 16, 1994.

49. Killian, "Southern White Laborers on Chicago's West Side, 204.

50. Bert Schloss, "The Uptown Community Area and the Southern White In-Migrant" Chicago Commission on Human Relations, 1957.

51. Joseph Kennedy, Chicago Police Department at a meeting in Uptown at the opening of the Chicago Southern Center in 1963. Southern Appalachian Archives (Box 284-3).

Chapter 4

Hillbilly Jungle and Hillbilly Heaven:
A Tale of Perceptions

Everybody was so afraid of the hillbillies. That is what was so wild. They were the safest group in the world. I was more afraid of Chicagoans.[1]

When anybody says anything about my being from the South I tell them "Damn right I'm from the South and I'm proud of it."[2]

Sarah Dotson managed to contact her husband who agreed to wait for her to arrive on the bus from West Virginia. She was unaware of the suspicion and hostility surrounding the arrival of the southerners. She had never heard of the previous research by Killian that found southerners to be an unwelcome addition to the Near West of Chicago in the 1940s.[3] By the time she arrived in 1959, tensions ran high between Chicagoans in Uptown and southern migrants. A reporter who was considering writing about southerners in Chicago was cautioned that she may not "come out alive" to write her story."[4] Chicagoans, who had never seen these newcomers, were influenced by media stereotypes that portrayed southerners as lazy, prone to violence, and unfit for work. Other articles described them as lawless drunks with improper hygiene, who engaged in sexual deviance.[5] By 1966, the labels had even reached southern newspapers. The *Charleston Gazette* wrote that "the fear of them [southern whites] in Chicago [was] greater than the Negro."[6] The appellation "hillbilly" that was negative for most Chicagoans became a badge of honor for southerners and was romanticized in Uptown.

Both daily newspapers like the *Tribune*, and community newspapers like the *Edgewater-Uptown News* contributed to the vilification of the southerner. This community press was the organ of local retail interests which had shifted north of the Loop in an effort to create decentralized retail centers in Chicago. The community press replaced the immigrant press which had flourished in the nineteenth and early twentieth centuries, and declined with assimilation of immigrants. More importantly the community press became the most consistent vehicle for local news in Chicago neighborhoods.[7]

As southern whites began to come to Uptown in large numbers during the 1950s, they learned that the press was beginning to project previously existing negative stereotypes about their arrival. An image of mountain life as squalid and degenerate has existed in American popular culture since the nineteenth century.[8] It did not help that they were often settling in substandard housing. In Baltimore a report painted a picture of southern white migrants that resembled a Charles Dickens novel using words like human misery and degradation to describe their conditions. Emaciated children were seen defecating in the apartment hallways, or filthy and covered with body sores. A family of seven lived in a converted furnace room in a basement with rats, and insects crawling over the author's shoes. This same report attributed slum conditions to the cultural attributes of the migrants:

> Many slums are, in fact, created by the tenants who are completely unaware of the urban living standards. With few exceptions, the housekeeping was appalling. One woman explained away the litter, the piles of unwashed clothes, the dirty dishes accumulated from many meals with 'I haven't done my weekend cleaning'. The odor of urine and filth were indescribable. [9]

The report went on to detail the degree to which southern migrants deliberately wrecked their apartments by removing spokes from banisters and breaking windows. Although the tone of the report was somewhat sympathetic to the plight of migrants in Baltimore, it added to the existing unfounded stereotypes about southern whites.

In Chicago newspapers helped to mobilize bias against southern white migrants. As with any stereotype, stories carried mixed elements of fact and fiction. Articles in the late 1950s stated that southern whites were, "at the bottom of the heap socially, morally, and mentally," and the cause for a rising crime rate in the city which caught the attention of the police. Some articles featured the scenes of the bloody hillbilly shooting brawls. Southerners were alleged to use "jungle tactics," were characterized as "savages and tribes" who were drunk "most of the time." Violence, a particular "odor," and "the awful racket from the bandstand characterized hillbilly taverns." Newspapers stated that men came to Chicago to get jobs and spend their money on "liquor, sex, and cars." According to press accounts, southerners were depraved, did not understand the idea of rape, or honor the idea of marriage or wedlock birth.[10] Incest, child brides, and clans of cousins who were unwilling to pay utility charges were all part of the stereotypical view of southern white culture. The home of migrants was a place of degradation and filth inhabited by uncaring adults who were bent on satisfying their own pleasure at the expense of their children. One journalist wrote that, "the hillbilly's home and family life experienced investigators say is the most depraved of any they have ever encountered, with no understanding of sanitation and health. Many children do not know who their parents are—and nobody cares."[11]

A jungle image was used in stories about the southern white neighborhood where crime was rampant and outsiders were potential victims. Fear reigned in Uptown as the *Edgewater Uptown News* reported that, thieves with "southern accents" terrorized residents, and roamed the streets committing petty crimes. The infamous southern drawl-the mark of ignorance and backwardness was rarely left out of an article about criminals from the South. From the articles, the reader was left with the impression that there was a hillbilly on every corner ready to pounce on unsuspecting Uptowners. One article featured, "James the Knife" from Alabama, who tried to rob a penniless janitor.[12] No one appeared safe from the southern crime wave. In 1957, the grisly murders of teens Barbara and Patricia Grimes whose nude and frozen bodies were found at Devil's Hill, were linked to Bennie "the Bum" Bedwell, "an ex-roustabout dishwasher, skid row bum—a resident of Chicago's new hillbilly jungle."[13] Bedwell fit the criminal profile of the half-wit, violent, miscreant, hillbilly created in the press.

> Most Chicagoans were shocked that hillbilly Bennie Bedwell couldn't read or write anything except his own name. Bennie isn't unique. There are thousands like him in Chicago today. There aren't enough police and truant officers to keep the hillbilly children in school. Gangs of young toughs molesting youths have caused many long time residents to move.[14]

Newspapers struck fear into long term residents by recording brawls involving bolo knives, and intoxicated "bail-jumping South Carolinians with southern accents" forcing their way into an apartment and beating a woman and her children.[15] Other articles described half-crazed hillbillies cutting each other and the police as they intervened. Still other stories reported that hillbilly teens were holding up truckers at gunpoint and robbing a defenseless couple out for an afternoon stroll.[16] Fear of urban newcomers is nothing new. Southern migrants in Uptown were but the newest urban group feared by citizens and the press. As such, they shared the stage with the Italians in the nineteenth century, and Mexican Americans and Cuban Marielitos in the twentieth century.[17]

By 1962, community tensions were running so high that a police chief defended the migrant's civic standing. In what would be a rare occurrence for the police in Uptown, Chief Fahey urged "understanding, patience, and cooperation" between longtime residents and the southerners. He pointed out that most southerners were not criminals.[18] A research report published at the time offered some support to Fahey's claims. While southern whites were not involved in arrests for serious crimes, they were more likely than most to be arrested for misdemeanors. It was estimated that southern whites made up about 20 percent of the population in the Town Hall district (of which Uptown was a part) but accounted for 35 percent of all arrests for disorderly conduct and intoxication in 1960 23percent of those arrested were from four states: Alabama, Kentucky, Tennessee, and West Virginia.[19] Most arrests for intoxication were made along Wilson Avenue, where numerous rowdy bars existed long before southerners had migrated to Uptown.

Moreover, it is unclear whether all those arrested were in fact from the South. The same report noted that "when a high percentage of persons in an area come from the South it is assumed that everyone in the neighborhood is southern." Inaccurate newspaper accounts added to the notorious reputation southern whites received. Some people were labeled "hillbilly" regardless of their place of birth.

It is likely that prejudice and stereotypes caused people to label offenders as southern regardless of where they were from. Suddenly everyone had a southern accent. This may explain the tenuous claims of an early unpublished report in which police were quoted as saying that 75 percent of their arrests and disturbances were caused by "hillbillies." However, none of the statements on crime were supported with analysis or arrest data.[20]

The police reacted to the claims of southern migrant criminality by enforcing strict curfews and loitering laws. There was constant tension and opposition between the police in Uptown and southern white migrants. One famous photo of Uptown during the 1960s shows a bare-chested, handcuffed southern white youth face down on the sidewalk. Around him stands a lone cop and an ominous crowd of southerners.[21] This inauspicious image characterized the relationship between the police and the southern migrants. Southerners recalled violent physical treatment carried out by police against them. Police broke up any group of men together on a corner. Sara Dotson's son Kenny from West Virginia, recalled southerners being treated as a different class of people."You weren't allowed to stand on the corner. Three or four of us would meet up talking on the street, you weren't allowed to do that. They'd say, scatter out or we'll haul you in."[22]

The police were suspicious about southern men gathering in groups because they assumed that they were planning illegal or disruptive acts. Kentuckian, Raleigh Campbell, a social worker in the Chicago Southern Center worked with migrant families in Uptown. He advised southerners against congregating for any reason because of the reputation of the police."The cops were really watching that sort of thing. I think that they [Chicago police] were as paranoid about hillbillies as southern cops are about blacks today—the same kind of blame."[23] By and large the nightstick was used to quell any protests by southerners if they were arrested. Merely having an accent was enough to provoke a response by police. "Oh gosh, as soon as you opened your mouth, you got a billy club up side your head."[24] Tennessean, Helen Elam was more specific about the physical and verbal abuse police administered to southern white migrants. "They called us dumb hillbillies and were very derogatory and would beat them [southern whites] when they were drunk or into some kind of situation. They did that to everyone. They [the police] didn't like anyone that they thought was a hillbilly."[25] Police violence seemed excessive and unnecessary, and did not escape the attention of observers at the time. There was an open season on anyone thought to be from the South. As a largely unorganized group southerners were fair game for police brutality. Again Raleigh Campbell spoke of the harsh treatment doled out to southerners by the police. As someone who worked closely with southern migrants, it was inappropriate treatment. "The police were beating our [southern] people in the head for no damn reason—just because they had a southern accent. [They'd] see them on the street corner and be just down right violent."[26] For Campbell, police violence went beyond simple physical encounters to include corruption. This was substantiated in Gitlin and Hollander's book. There were unofficial reports of police planting drugs in order to make arrests to discourage southerners from organizing to protest.[27]

Others related similar stories of involvement with police, ranging from beatings to rape. When I interviewed Donald Powell, described a fight that he had been involved in. When the police arrived he ran. His two friends were not so lucky. Powell stated that when police arrested them they intentionally left their hand cuffs loose to encourage them to escape. Powell watched from another location. "They [his friends] was the one's that was playing cards with me. So the cops handcuffed them together, but they left Bo's handcuffs real loose; real smart cops, you know so he could slip his hand out and run, so he could shoot him. Bo made it around the corner and Billie didn't; the cops was shooting at him and a bullet hit him right here [gesturing to his head] and grazed his head and knocked him out, left a scar."[28] Another woman recalled the beating her son received by police and the suspicious outcome of the police investigation. After the incident she never trusted the police.

> My youngest son was beaten by a policeman on his back, his spine. He suffers to this day. I took him to Emergency. I had a Polaroid camera and I took pictures of his back. I turned them over to internal affairs. Well, I trusted the police in those days. She [the internal affairs officer] wanted the pictures. I never got them back. I did get a letter saying that there was insufficient evidence.[29]

During this time, charges of police misconduct were common in many American cities. Police reacted violently to protesters at the Democratic convention in Chicago, and there were violent encounters in Detroit, Newark and Los Angeles. For their part, the urban police felt under siege as well by urban crime, war protesters and militant groups. Eventually this reached a tragic climax in Uptown when police fatally shot one of two brothers that were arguing under the elevated tracks on Wilson Avenue. Southerners were shocked by the accusation that the man was laying down when he received the fatal pistol shots. One migrant recalled this incident in an interview:

> I had a friend. One of her boys was killed by the police right over here on Wilson under the el [elevated tracks] because they were fighting. Somebody called the police and they shot him five times. After he was down. The cops stood there and pumped five bullets into that man.[30]

Southerners grew more suspicious and began to distrust the police or any public officials. A code of silence emerged, which exacerbated police-community relations.[31] Chicago Southern Center's Raleigh Campbell feared that this would lead to more violence. Campbell was worried that the police would to more harsh methods of interrogation, or simply ignore calls reported by southerners. For their part, the police resented the tendency of southerners to solve problems without the help of police or refuse to cooperate. When I interviewed officers who had patrolled Uptown during this time this was apparent in their responses. "Crimes by southerners were never reported in those days. The victims and offenders knew each other and would exchange places the next week. When a call came in about a stabbing, there was no cooperation from 'um [southerners]. They'd take care of it themselves."[32]

The situation, however, was more complex, and potentially explosive. Prejudice and violent treatment reinforced the negative impression of law enforcement. This inhibited southerners from using traditional methods, such as calling the police, to solve disputes. Like any group who perceives themselves as the target of hostility, southern migrants withdrew and ceased cooperating with the police. The community became internally self regulating. Instead of risking violence from police or being singled out for harsh treatment, the situation was handled by the southerners in Uptown. Raleigh Campbell shed light on the strained relations between the police and southern migrants. His view is less cynical than the officer quoted above who emphasized the absence of legitimate alternatives."They [southerners] got so they would not call the police. They knew that they'd probably get discriminated against. They knew that the police would probably beat them over the head. If they had problems, they'd handle it themselves."[33]

The police complained that they received negative and unwelcome treatment from southern whites. They claimed that southerners turned on them when they tried to intervene in domestic disputes and that the victim and the offenders often preferred to settle disputes without the police. The police responded by exerting more pressure on southerners in the form of curfews and restrictions on gathering. The situation fed on itself until police-community relations spiraled out of control leading to protests and picketing by southern migrants. Protesters carried signs reading "hillbilly power" in front of the local police station.[34] To the police and longtime wealthier residents, southern whites were the problem. Moreover to protest against the police, who were increasingly seen in negative terms in media coverage from non-violent Civil Rights protesters in the South to urban anti-war protesters, invited even more repressive measures. It was futile and unwise. The police wielded unrestrained use of force that they were too willing to use against the opposition.

Uptown was also inheriting problems of its past evolution as a center for entertainment and vice. Community newspapers reflected a near hysteria from residents. Outraged citizens lamented the newcomer's arrival, and criticized their behavior. A sort of moral panic that was heightened by press accounts of southern migrants emerged.[35] Alcohol was often cited as a key problem and source of neighborhood decline. Residents believed that Uptown was saturated with bars and liquor stores where southern migrants were the main patrons. Many felt that the cause for broken homes, delinquency, and adultery lay in the bottle and the hillbilly's uncontrollable penchant for booze. Editorials lashed out at city and state officials for issuing permits that allowed taverns to remain open late. Dissipation and filth were linked to southern "drunks of both sexes, loud screeching jukeboxes of idiotic music, arguments, knifings, crime, empty whiskey, and beer containers in doorways." More reform minded residents sought control of the liquor stores and their ability to deliver the "mental and bodily poison" to the homes of southerners.[36] Citizens were concerned that southern migrants would have a detrimental effect on property values in Uptown. One long-time resident of Uptown reflected these sentiments by delineating the process of neighborhood decline at a meeting of civic leaders.

> I have lived here for forty-five years. This was a silk stocking neighborhood. I saw it change. I remember being alerted by real estate people and letter carriers when this influx of southern people began that they would come in and rent an apartment for two people and in the morning the landlord would find eight or ten there sleeping on the floor. The problem here is terrific.[37]

This type of criticism ignores the larger structural forces that were affecting property values in Uptown, and did not acknowledge that the seeds of neighborhood decline had preceded the arrival of southern whites. Uptown had been known for its night life, taverns and liquor consumption as early as the 1920s. The deteriorated housing and low rents that attracted southerners to Uptown had existed before their arrival.

Southerners were also linked with neighborhood blight through their association with shabby or abandoned automobiles.[38] Estimates had police towing over 100 picked-over wrecks a month and thirteen hundred a year from Uptown streets in 1965.[39] Citizens were outraged at the number of southerners who repaired their cars at the curb. When it was too cold to repair them in the winter cars in various states of disrepair lined the streets. More affluent residents openly criticized the mayor and city officials for apparent tolerance. This was further proof of decline. One citizen expressed a cynical view of this at a community meeting about southern migrants when he stated that he had "suggested that the Uptown Chamber of Commerce send the State of Tennessee a new coat of arms which would consist of two men with their heads under the engine part of an automobile and their backsides sticking up."[40] In his eyes, the sight of men working on a car degraded the neighborhood. However, southern men had no other recourse than to repair their car themselves. If men had no mechanical skills, shade-tree mechanics were willing to repair their cars for less than the cost of a legitimate garage. Southerners also trusted someone from the neighborhood repairing their cars. This informal cash economy also maintained members of the migrant community. When I interviewed Donald Powell, he stated that everyone abandoned their cars if they didn't have the money to take them to a garage to have them repaired. "Everybody does that" [abandons their car] "If it tears up and does not work well, if they can't, if they don't know, you know, somebody you know where they can get paid for it to come tow it in."[41]

Angry citizens such as the one above also failed to realize the importance of the car as a means of transportation. It was indispensable to get to factory jobs which were located in the suburbs of Chicago. As long as southerners had their car they could return home and maintain family ties. "As long as I had good transportation back and forth home maybe taking our two weeks vacation in the summer, you know, go home on the weekend. [We would] go on Friday afternoon and come back on Sunday afternoon. I was pretty much satisfied."[42] Southern migrants needed their cars because it was a connection to home. A car enabled people to remain in the North by providing the option to return home. In a general way, the automobile represented freedom and individuality, mainstream American cultural values. In a specific way the automobile has particular cultural significance in the South, exhibited in such films as *Thunder Road*. Set in eastern Kentucky, the film glorified exploits of bootleggers outrunning government agents in fast cars risking their lives for their load of liquor. In addition, the health of the U.S. economy was increasingly dependent on the auto.[43]

Officials close to the migrants sometimes intervened on their behalf. Some felt that the problems in the community should not be attributed to southern migrants alone. In one case, Bob Mulligan, director of the Uptown Hull House, pleaded that the newcomers were the "key to our future." Mulligan reminded Uptowners that migrants were the economic backbone of Chicago and urged the community to accept them. He also reminded readers that much of Uptown's blight and deterioration had preceded the arrival of southern migrants. "They [southern migrants] don't get into a community unless it has already started to deteriorate and landlords have made many conversions here. They cut up apartments and pile more and more people into them."[44] Mulligan was reminding readers of the *Edgewater-Uptown News*, of the mass conversation of large apartments begun by owners as early as World War II in Uptown.

Those professionals who worked closely with migrants refuted the notion that all migrant homes were filthy. Tom Moore, formerly of the Boys Club in Uptown, made routine visits to migrant apartments throughout the period. In his words, migrant homes differed from the widespread media portrayals. They were "modest, but clean. For the most part there was a great deal of cleanliness."[45] The cycle of decline that citizens were alarmed by had started before the arrival of southern migrants. The angry citizens were witnessing the effects of forces that preceded the arrival of migrants from the South. These newcomers may have been guilty of being poor, but residents criticizing their poverty failed to realize larger forces that made Uptown attractive to the lower income of all groups.

Beneath the crime-infested and filthy conditions reported in newspapers and trumpeted by residents, southern white migrants were generating a thriving community in Uptown. While negative stereotypes and public scrutiny heightened the controversy surrounding their arrival, interviews with migrants revealed a complex community interwoven by social networks based on their southern origins, kinship and friendship. They took pride in their neighborhood and rejected their association with neighborhood decline. Moreover, they adopted creative ways to avoid police harassment and an unwelcome reception. However derogatory the term hillbilly may have been, many southerners adopted it as a familiar way to describe their neighborhood in Chicago. Uptown was hillbilly heaven. The fact that southerners appropriated the term reflects a certain understanding of their identity as outsiders. While interviewing Donald Powell I asked him his understanding of living in the North and about the meaning of the term, hillbilly. He stated that he was aware of what others thought of southerners. "Well, that they called us living here on Wilson and Clifton [Streets] living together, all hillbillies." I then asked him whether he thought that his was an insult or a favorable appellation. He stated, "Um, I don't think. Gosh, it's the truth it was hillbilly heaven. It was hillbillies, southerners, you know."[46]

Indeed others began to recognize this and began to profit from it by publicizing their association with southerners in Uptown. Taverns regularly booked bands advertised as being "hillbilly" in the *Edgewater-Uptown News*. Tex Carter's Lounge advertised as the "New Hillbilly Heaven" booked Russell Morris billed as "The Hillbilly's Friend." Groups like The Westernaires frequently reminded Uptowners of the presence of large numbers of southerners.[47] The Drift Inn was also noted for its hillbilly and mountain music with groups like The Alabama Playboys featuring Rabon Sanders who recorded "You Tore Your Playhouse Down" in 1959.[48] Jukeboxes in these taverns were filled with western and hillbilly music. Uptown was one of the largest stops for those servicing jukeboxes with country music. By the 1950s one store in Uptown sold disproportionately more country music than any other place in the city.[49] By 1965, over 50 percent of the records sold in Chicago were country western, and at least one radio station had switched to a country format. The Rivoli Theatre, long closed, reopened as a successful country dance hall featuring performers such as Johnny Cash, Buck Owens, and Ray Price.[50] As James Gregory has argued, music is a critical cultural medium. It is a source of identity for many subgroups in society. Song lyrics carried meaning relating to the experiences of migrants, and often reaffirmed their sense of belonging to a group.[51] Music was also one of the most recognizable elements of southern culture in Uptown.

Geographic concentration facilitated community, and provided security for those unfamiliar with the city. Living in close proximity to other family members encouraged solidarity. If life was kin-centered at their places of origin, so was it in Chicago. Kinship gave migrants a sense of security because one could rely on family members in time of need. Kinfolk symbolized a sense of belonging and home. Helen Elam remembered that her mother felt a sense of community because many of her relatives were living in buildings within a one-block radius. Although she never thought of Chicago as being home in the sense of belonging, she felt secure knowing her relatives were close.

> She [her mother] never considered Chicago in general a permanent home, but she considered that building [912 West Montrose] a permanent place because our family was over there on that street. [Montrose avenue between Hazel and Sheriden Avenues] Three of her brothers and sisters. There were two on Montrose there, down further toward the right over across the street, and my other uncle and aunt were across the street over on Agatite. This neighborhood from Magnolia to Clarendon was solid white and southern.[52]

Relatives watched each other's children, or took them to taverns to play the juke box while adults worked. During the height of the migration in the middle fifties, there were blocks of buildings entirely occupied by southern migrants. Streets like Montrose, and Kenmore, were packed with southerners. Raleigh Campbell remembered walking home from the Chicago Southern Center counting licence plates from the South trying to guess which county they were from. "I was always amused. I was out on the streets a lot in Uptown, and you'd see this block with cars from Tennessee and that one with cars from Kentucky and you knew where people were from by that. All Kentucky people were together. They were guests, or relatives, or living here."[53] A municipal report that was issued by the Chicago Commission on Human Relations in 1957confirmed clustering patterns in the areas above. Kinship played a significant role in the social organization of southerners in Uptown.

> It is not uncommon to find medium-sized rooming houses of ten to thirty apartments, occupied 80 to 100 percent with southern whites. Whenever we found one southern family, we were almost certain to find a great many other southern families, many of whom were blood relatives or from a common community from the South. Major concentrations were found in the area between Broadway and Racine on the west. Some streets such as Clifton Street, Racine Avenue and Hazel Street, certain parts of Winthrop, Kenmore Avenues and Sheriden Road are fairly solidly occupied by southern white migrants.[54]

Southerners were not accustomed to densely populated urban neighborhoods. However, with the unwelcome reception southerners received, living in close proximity offered southern migrants a psychological cushion. Concentration facilitated security, a sense of community, and social and occupational networks. It eased the transition to city life. The thousands of southerners coming to Uptown transformed it into something familiar. There were kinfolk with whom to exchange news of home, taverns to frequent, family picnics by the lake, and weekly card games. People from the same town in the South met in Chicago for the first time. Others married fellow southerners only to later find out that they had common friends, and in some cases, spouses who knew each other's families back home. West Virginian, Violet McKnight, recalled how this happened after she settled as a single woman in Uptown:

> I met my husband right here in Uptown. He was from the same area as I was in West Virginia. I was from Mann and he was from Williamson. I knew his people back there, but I didn't know him personally. He worked as a miner back home and left years before I did to get away from that work. He came here and got a job in a factory. We had four children here—two boys and two girls.[55]

Sarah Dotson loved the neighborhood, the housing, and amenities in apartments. "It was just a nice neighborhood, really nice, you know. You could almost lay down [sleep] with your doors open, when I come into the neighborhood."[56]

Migrants also felt at home with the presence of southerners in many of the neighborhood businesses. If you went into the New Yankee Grill or Goldblatts department store, you were likely to be greeted by a waitress or clerk from back home. This was very important for preserving identity and building community among migrants. Continued contact with southerners reinforced a southern identity. Virginia recalled moving to Uptown and being surrounded with southerners who helped her maintain her southern identity.

> Since there were southern people here and I worked with them everyday, I didn't lose anything. I was still southern. I had started losing my southern accent, [at another place of employment] but when I began to work with southerners again I just went back into that role, that southern talk, that old hillbilly slang, you know.[57]

Virginia felt like she belonged in Uptown. She also experienced a change in what it meant to be from the South. Being from the South meant protecting your community and defending others in the community. Back home people rarely thought about what it meant to be southern. In Chicago an identity emerged, due in part, to the hostile reception. This unity extended throughout Uptown among southern migrants during this time. Extended kin performed a vital role in the social network of the community. The presence of family members and kin in the same block or building lessened the sense of uprootedness and provided a measure of security.

Whereas local churches were not adopted by migrants, the tavern became a primary social institution around which southern migrants organized social networks. The tavern has been recognized by historians and sociologists as being a central community institution. Taverns especially have been an integral part of the structure of social networks that develop among the lower classes.[58] Continued police harassment and hostile treatment drove many men into bars to socialize. The bar was a place where they could gather without the fear of police harassment. Taverns served an essential function in the web of social networks and relationships for southern men. Similar to the Bodegas in Puerto Rican communities, it was in the tavern that men found out about jobs, friends back home, and other news.[59]

Although not the rule, a few southerners became entrepreneurs. Alabamians, like Charles and Janice Mitchell, who came in 1956, owned a bowling alley and a neighborhood pool hall in Uptown. The Webbs owned a grocery store that carried familiar items from home such as sweet milk. Though not in Uptown, Helen Elam's uncle opened the Blue Moon bar after coming to Chicago in the forties. He had a tip jar marked for a college fund for Helen on the bar. Helen remembered her uncle being protective and insisted that she attend college.

> I had my uncle's bar, the Blue Moon. We went over there to play pool. Back then you could go out by yourself at night. I used to help behind the bar serving drinks. And the tip money went into a jar for college. None of the patrons were allowed to bother us. My uncle was very old fashioned.[60]

More often than not, tavern owners in Uptown simply changed their establishments to suit their new clientele. Juke boxes were re-stocked with southern music. The Drift Inn at 5138 Broadway advertised country and western musicians and featured a Wednesday night jam session. Donald Powell went to Andy's tavern broke and was allowed to run a tab. At other places like the Red Dog bar he had a $50.00 per week limit on alcohol. On Friday, Red Dog's owner, a Kentuckian, cashed the patron's checks and took his share out. He had two other bars in the neighborhood frequented by southerners. Southerners considered taverns their own havens from an often hostile world. The bar was their own territory, a place where they knew everyone else. In the words of an observer at the time, the tavern was their hangout. It offered security and safety against outsiders. "You had to be careful. They became suspicious of those they didn't know. Undercover police were working the bars."[61]

Street life was vital to southern migrants. Women and men gathered outside in the summer under large trees. Social space was used in an effective way to adapt to police harassment. Migrants tended to congregate on stoops or in the space in front of their buildings. Groups were less likely to be broken up by police if they were in the yard of their apartment building. This was particularly attractive as an escape from the hot cramped apartments on summer evenings. Large trees became the focal point of the buildings. Groups of four or five people sat on porches or stoops, or on the numerous fire escapes used for back porches. These gatherings were a way to exchanging information or for coping with problems in the city. Women preferred friends' houses to exchange information and socialize. They were the eyes and ears of the street while their husbands were at work. This wove together a network of information about the community and kept others updated when they were away from the neighborhood during trips back home in the South.

Southern white migrants to Chicago shared similar experiences with other urban migrant groups in history. The process of urban migration, settlement, and community building was common to southern white migrants as well as other urban migrants. Southern white migrants built a community in an urban port of entry in light of an unwelcome reception. Part of this sense of community was bound up in the migration experience itself, events unfolding at the port of entry, and the meaning that the migrants attached to it. The atavistic image of mountain folk that was imputed on white southerners influenced public opinion, and created a citywide image of southern white migrants as undesirable newcomers to Chicago.

The migration experience is important in understanding the emergence of a distinct identity among southerners in the North. It separated southern white migrants from their brethren who remained in the South. The process made southern whites in Chicago culturally distinct. Similar to the unique Mexican-American cultural identity that evolved in Los Angeles, southern white identity evolved in the historical context of migration and larger social forces that existed at their destination. As such, this identity is continually in flux.[62] Migrants clustered together and united against the community opposition that surrounded their arrival in Uptown. Though kinship was a primary bond, southern heritage emerged as a mechanism for unity. The presence of a "critical mass" of southerners and the fact that no single locality from the South dominated contributed to this identity. In this way a unique cultural identity developed which was southern in a mythic sense. What being "southern" meant in Chicago was different from what it meant in the South where regional or local appellations and culture prevailed. For example, a county affiliation may have meant more about one's connection than the fact that they were from the South, or even West Virginia for that matter. Recent immigrants from Mexico are much more concerned with their region of origin, being from San Luis Potosi for example than they are from being from Mexico. This involves the particular regional culture that this entails. However, to most Americans their identity is viewed in monolithic terms, as being Mexican. Just as many immigrant groups in the past experienced a sort of emergent ethnicity in the United States, southern migrants were becoming acutely aware of being from the South in Chicago.

Southern white migrant identity was first encouraged from without by forces in their community of settlement. Whereas the media, community leaders, and the police labeled southerners as undesirable and viewed being southern as a stigma, southerners embraced their heritage with pride and made it a prerequisite for unity. Just as values, experience and character were inherent in the Okie subculture in California, Southern whites in Chicago adopted similar traits in Chicago. With that said, to romanticize the southern white migrants in Uptown would be inaccurate as well. Doing so raises questions about the validity of the media, police and residents. Southern whites were involved in crime. The housing problems and general decline were real. However, to hold southern whites responsible for these problems is illogical. The urban decline and ensuing social problems had their roots in larger social and structural forces affecting communities throughout the nation during the time period examined. Neighborhood blight had its roots in the early conversion of buildings in Uptown to single rooms, the retail boom, that had begun to fade, and wages in Chicago that were in the initial stages of slipping. Labeling southerners as inherently crime prone, and degenerate heightened the crisis atmosphere and created a moral panic in some ways. This nascent identity would be facilitated by the opening of the Chicago Southern Center in 1963. Driven by the aim of aiding in urban, adjustment the center fostered a generic southern identity through common themes drawn from the South.

Notes

1. Personal interview by the author with Raleigh Campbell, former director of the Chicago Southern Center, 1964–1966, 5 August 1995.
2. Lewis Killian, "Southern White Laborers in Chicago's West Side." (Unpublished Ph.D. diss., University of Chicago, 1949): 182.
3. Killian "Southern White Laborers in Chicago's West Side."

4. Norma Lee Browning, "Girl Reporter Visits Jungles of Hillbillies." *Chicago Daily Tribune,* 3 March 1957, 1(N).

5. "When Whites Migrate from the South,"*U.S. News and World Report,* 14 October 1963: 70-73.

6. "Appalachians in a Hostile World," *Charleston Gazette-Mail,* October 9, 1966.

7. Robert Park., *The Immigrant Press and Its Control* (New York: Harper, 1920); Morris Janowitz, *The Community Press in an Urban Setting* (Chicago: University of Chicago Press, 1964).

8. Henry D. Shapiro, *Appalachia on Our Mind: The Southern Mountains and Mountaineers in the American Consciousness, 1870–1920* (Chapel Hill: University of North Carolina Press, 1978), 59–84.

9. National Council of Jewish Women."The Unaccepted Baltimoreans: A Report on the White Southern Rural Migrants." (Unpublished report by the Baltimore section of the National Council of Jewish Women, May 1961): 3.

10. Norma Lee Browning, "Girl Reporter Visits Jungles of Hillbillies.*"Chicago Daily Tribune,* 3 March 1957 and "New Breed of Migrants City Problem."*Chicago Daily Tribune,* 4 March 1957.

11. "Girl Reporter Visits Jungles of Hillbillies."

12. "James 'the Knife' From Alabama to Stay Here 30 Days." *Uptown News,* July 5, 1961, 1(N).

13. "Murder 'Won't Out,' Paper Concludes After Investigation." *Uptown News,* 21 May 1957, 1(N).

14. "Girl Reporter Visits Jungles of Hillbillies."

15."Brawl Ends in Blood When Man is Sliced With Bolo Knife."*Edgewater-Uptown News,* 28 February1961, 1(N) "South Carolinian Jumps Bail After Assault Charge." *Edgewater-Uptown News,* 28 March 1961, 1(N). "3 Slug Mother and Hit Children." *Edgewater-Uptown News,* 11 April 1961, 4(N).

16. "Doesn't Pay to Play Rough Here." *Edgewater-Uptown News,* March 6, 1962; "Walk Ends as Gunmen Take Cash," *Edgewater Uptown News,* 24 September 1963, 1(N). "Trucker Robbed of $2,000 by Teen," *Edgewater Uptown News,* 26 February1963, 1(N).

17. For an Italian example see, Patrick Gallo, *Old Bread New Wine: A Portrait of Italian Americans (Chicago: Nelson-Hall, 1981).* For a Mexican American example see, Alfredo Mirande Mirande, "El Bandido: The evolution of Images of Chicano Criminality," in *The Chicano Experience: An Alternative Perspective* (Notre Dame, Indiana: University of Notre Dame Press, 1985) For the Marialito example see, Alejandro Portes and Alex Stepick, "A Year to Remember: Mariel," in *City on the Edge: The Transformation of Miami* (Berkley: University of California Press, 1994).

18. "Town Hall Chief Defends Migrants." *Edgewater Uptown News,* 13 February 1962, 1 (N).

19. Harry H. Woodward, "The Southern White Migrant in Lakeview" (Appendix 3, Table 4) Published by the Lakeview Citizen's Council, 1962.

20. Bert Schloss, "The Uptown Community and the Southern White In-Migrant." (Unpublished report, Chicago Commission on Human Relations, 1957).

21. Gitlin and Hollander, *Uptown: Poor Whites in Chicago.*

22. Personal interview with Kenny Dotson, 20 June 1994.

23. Campbell interview.

24. Personal interview by the author with Virginia Bowers, 18 March 1994.

25. Personal interview by the author with Helen Elam, 18 December 1994.

26. Campbell interview.

27. This was reported widely in Gitlin and Hollander, *Uptown: Poor Whites in Chicago*. Another account emerged during while interviewing Raleigh Campbell for this chapter about the police planting drugs on a local clergyman working with southern white youth in order to remove him from the neighborhood.

28. Personal interview by the author with Donald Powell, 28 June 1994.

29. Interviewee wished to remain anonymous.

30. Interviewee wished to remain anonymous.

31. Campbell interview.

32. Personal interview by the author with Sergeant Robert Johnson, Chicago Police Department, 14 February 1994.

33. Campbell interview.

34. "Appalachians in a Hostile World," *Charleston Gazette-Mail*, 9 October 1966.

35. For a Mexican American example and usage of this term see Joan Moore. *Going Down to the Barrio: Homeboys and Homegirls in Change* (Philadelphia: Temple University Press, 1991).

36. "Keep Booze Sales Down." *Edgewater-Uptown News*, 4 June 1964.

37. Transcription of a community meeting held in connection with the opening of the Chicago Southern Center, 7 November 1963. Southern Appalachian Archives, Berea College, Berea, Ky.

38. "Retired Warrior Battles Abandoned Cars in 48th,"*Edgewater Uptown News*, 20 August 1963.

39. "War on Junk Autos Launched in Uptown," *Edgewater-Uptown News*, 22 March 1966.

40. Minutes to a meeting on the opening of the Chicago Southern Center. Southern Appalachian Archives. (Box 284-3) Hutchinson Library, Berea College.

41. Powell interview.

42. Bowers interview.

43. Jim Patterson, *Great Expectations: The United States, 1945-1974*. (New York: Oxford University Press), 70.

44. "Newcomers Key to Our Future." *Edgewater-Uptown News*, 17 December 1963.

45. Interview with Tom Moore, April 20, 1994.

46. Powell Interview.

47. *Edgewater-Uptown News*, 21 February 1956.

48. <http://rcs.law.emory.edu/rcs/artists/s/sand3000.htm>(December 30, 2006).

49. Chad Berry, *Southern Migrants Northern Exiles* (Urbanna: University of Illinois Press),158.

50. "Now it's Country-Western Music Public Wants," *Edgewater-Uptown News,* 2, June 1965, 2(N).

51. James N. Gregory. *American Exodus: The Dust Bowl Migration and Okie Culture in California*. (New York: Oxford University Press), 234.

52. Elam interview.

53. Campbell interview.

54. "The Uptown Community and the Southern White In-Migrant." Chicago Commission on Human Relations, 1957.

55. Personal interview by the author with Violent McKnight, 22 June 1994.

56. Sarah Dotson interview.

57. Bowers interview.

58. Arthur Shostak. *Blue Collar Aristocrats* (Englewood Cliffs, New Jersey: Prentice Hall, 1964); Perry Duis, *The Saloon and Public Drinking in Chicago and Boston, 1820-1920* (Urbana: University of Illinois Press, 1983); Elijah Anderson. *A Place on the Corner* (Chicago: University of Chicago Press, 1978).
59. For a discussion of the Bodegas see Virginia Sánchez-Korrol. *From Colonia to Community*. (Berkeley: University of California Press, 1983).
60. Elam interview.
61. Personal interview by the author with Fred Lickerman, former director of the Robert R. McCormick Boys Club, 5 April 1994.
62. Mexican American identity in Los Angeles is discussed in George Sánchez, *Becoming Mexican American Ethnicity Culture and Identity in Los Angeles, 1900-1945.* (New York: Oxford University Press, 1993).

Chapter 5

Unity, Community, and the Chicago Southern Center

> The southern migrant in Chicago is notoriously difficult to help. He doesn't organize or attend meetings. Nor does he do any of the other things underprivileged minority groups are supposed to do. These are the facts of Uptown that often puzzle social workers and make the migrant alien in the midst of middle-class America. [1]

> The trouble with the social agencies is that they keep coming around trying to sell us something. Almost none of them ever bothers to ask what we need.[2]

While Sarah Dotson and Donald Powell easily found work after coming to Uptown, others were ill-prepared for employment and the rigors of life in Chicago. Poverty, poor health, and school truancy of southern migrants alarmed social agencies. For many migrants, the American dream or even simple sustenance was not materializing. Some were caught in the cycle of unstable work and inadequate wages brought by temporary work or day labor. Added to this were the continued media portrayals of migrants unprepared for urban life. In one instance the New York Times ran a picture of half-clothed, barefoot children, playing atop the shell of a car on cinder blocks.[3] Even local leaders in Kentucky were caught up in the frenzy and preoccupation with the urban hillbilly.[4] Although much help was available the private and public groups had little success in providing aid to migrants.[5] Those seeking to help the migrants complained that they were unable to reach them or that southerners refused their efforts. Some of this reluctance stemmed from the hostile reception they received in Uptown. After police harassment, stereotyping, and negative media scrutiny, southern whites were suspicious of officialdom. An organization having roots in the South had more success than other social service agencies.

The Chicago Southern Center (CSC) succeeded in part because of its emphasis on southern culture and identity. This stemmed from its connection with the Council of the Southern Mountains (CSM).[6] Activities at the CSC were family focused and stressed job placement, counseling and cultural activities. The Chicago Boys Club and the Glenmary Sisters's Appalachian Study Center also experienced success helping southern migrants.

One of the first social institutions to experience the impact of southern migrants were the schools in Uptown. Beginning in the 1950s, school principals recorded turnover rates as high as 150 percent. One school official during the time commented that, "kids were coming in and out of schools like turnstiles."[7] The high truancy and low retention began to take a toll on the quality of education being offered to rest of the students. The workload of the teachers increased as a result the retention problems. Teachers complained that migrant children were slowing down other students because they were not prepared academically. Other teachers argued that they were having to repeat lesson plans because of the high absenteeism in their classes.[8] Businesses were slowly becoming alarmed at the rate of migration, and the future costs to the area. One idea centered on slowing down the exodus from the South by boosting economic development in the regions losing population. A company memo circulated at Combined Insurance in Uptown predicted that millions of southern whites were ready to converge on Chicago, and proposed industrial development patterned after Operation Bootstrap in Puerto Rico to avert "disaster" in Uptown.[9]

Reports published by local civic groups, citizen's councils, and City Hall offered explanations and suggestions for anyone in contact with southern migrants. The Boys Clubs found children desperately in need of medical and dental care. Rates of T.B. and lead poisoning soared throughout the fifties and sixties in Uptown. Southern children were sometimes poisoned from eating the peeling paint from the decrepit apartment walls, once home to upscale urbanites.[10] Mayor Daley was also concerned with the influx of migrants. To show his commitment to understand the problems faced by all migrants in Chicago, he elevated the Chicago Commission on Human Relations to department-level status in January of 1957 and became the first public agency of its kind in the country. Late that same year, the Mayor's Committee on New Residents issued a report in conjunction with the Welfare Council of Metropolitan Chicago about all migrants to Chicago. The report estimated that there were twenty to fifty thousand southern whites in Chicago.[11]

Community leaders in Uptown were uneasy with the presence of southern white migrants. Of major concern by employers and school officials was the tendency of southern whites to frequently return home to the South. In 1957 the Chicago Commission on Human Relations produced a report on southern white migrants in Uptown. The investigators who compiled the report interviewed employers, residents, and southern newcomers, and concluded that southern whites contributed to the social disorganization of the area because they were "an unstable and unsettled element." The investigators felt their sentimentality about home and the lack of integration into urban institutions encouraged a "psychology of instability and impermanence." The report recommended that southern whites be assisted in securing employment, decent housing and acceptance by the community.[12] Many assumed that these social problems had unique cultural origins that were common to the South. Southern migrants were thought to lack the cultural and religious underpinnings of middle class America. Journalist Clarus Backus commented that, "the hillbilly as a whole works to live and regards labor of any kind as a necessary evil, a means to an end at best."[13] Southerners were thought to be a unique hybrid of an American lacking the work ethic common to those readers in the expanding suburbs. The southern family differed significantly from the fictional families in television shows such as *Father Knows Best* or *Leave It to Beaver*. Juxtaposed with the carloads of hillbilly families that Americans watched arriving on the evening news were the ideal middle class families on television. Southern white migrants were compared to these television ideals in spite of how far from reality they were. Most of those commenting on southern white migrants in the media, or in official reports argued that these newcomers could begin their ascent into the middle class if they changed their values brought from the hills. It was a sort of push to assimilate the hillbilly. In Milton Gordon's terms, cultural assimilation was essential if southern migrants were to take advantage of an opportunity structure that had benefitted other white ethnic groups in the past.[14] As a result, concerted efforts to accomplish this were launched in most cities in which migrants were arriving. Chicago was no exception.

In July of 1957, forty-three neighborhood and civic leaders gathered in the Sheridan-Plaza Hotel to discuss solutions to neighborhood decline. The Uptown Chicago Commission sponsored the meeting. The vast array of members included representatives from Mayor Daley's office, judges, prominent business leaders, church officials, and educators, and a choral group of southern white children from St. Paul's Church and Day School who sang for the assembly. Chief among the concerns of this group was transiency among the new arrivals from the South. Using the survey results from the Commission on Human Relations report, they discussed how to alleviate problems associated with southern migrants. The group proposed a five-point program to assist southern migrants in Uptown: 1. Seek out and develop new leaders from among the new groups; 2. Solicit funds to establish an office with a full time professional staff to make contacts with southerners and aid them with housing and employment; 3. Inform landlords of buildings occupied by southern whites about health and welfare facilities; 4. Begin a transiency and pupil turnover study; 5. Continue to lobby to bring more youth services and welfare agencies to Uptown.[15]

School officials at the Sheridan-Plaza meeting expressed concerns over high rates of classroom turnover among southern children. They felt that mountain culture determined attitudes toward school, including poor attendance and low levels of performance. Newspaper articles combined with official reports mutually reinforced the notion that mountain culture had "no strong tradition and respect for the value of formal education. The cultural traditions consider a little reading and writing the goal of formal education." This report went on to argue that culture rather than native ability accounted for low levels of education in the hills of Kentucky.[16] Stockton, Stewart, and Goudy elementary schools in Uptown were ports of entry for a transient element, which made up over half of the student population. In Goudy and Stewart almost half the student body came from stable homes. The high transiency rate was limited to 50 or 60 percent of the students who were newcomers to the city.[17] The observers felt that the solution rested in changing the parents' cultural values toward education if migrants were not to become a burden to society. To accomplish this value shift school officials felt that southern migrants would have to "surrender deep-seated attitudes and convictions and finally abandon one culture and acquire the characteristics of another."[18]

Citizens, social, and civic leaders discussed the evolution of migrant turnover in schools during community meetings. School officials felt that the frequent return trips back home in the South had a disruptive effect on migrant children and their performance in school. Citizens were worried about the overall effect that migration was having on the neighborhood. By the biggest concern came from the educators in Uptown.

> In the earlier days school principals complained to me. They said, 'Look, they come in here on Tuesday and register. Wednesday they come to school. Thursday they are on their way to Tennessee. They arrive here the next Monday and by Wednesday we don't hear from them anymore. They come one or two more days and by the next Wednesday they have moved out of the neighborhood.' I was invited over to a meeting at the Gramae-Stewart school. [The principal] stated that a child who was there more than six weeks was an old timer.[19]

Similar concerns were expressed in other cities with southern white migrant populations. Berea College sociologist Perley Ayer, executive secretary of the Council of the Southern Mountains, spent a sabbatical in Columbus Ohio observing southern white migrants. He found schools overloaded with migrants and excessive dropout rates. It was Ayer's conclusion that the hostile reception that most migrants received led to "shuttle migration." Migrants returned home frequently seeking the emotional warmth that home provided. This resulted in high absenteeism at work and school.[20]

In one of the few surviving documents on Baltimore, the National Council on Jewish women conducted a survey of southern white migrants in 1961. Although filled with stereotypes, it contained some keen observations about the challenges faced by schools. In one example, an elementary school with a total enrolment of 400 was expected to have 1,500 address changes by June. In another school 50 percent of the pupils had spent less than half the school year at one school. The author of the report attributed high truancy rates to a cultural attitude that did not value education or looked on it as a necessary evil. The report found that emotional problems also plagued migrant children due to the immorality, violence, and disorder in their homes. Teachers argued that they were unable to communicate with children because their speech patterns were more like Elizabethan than standard American English.[21] School officials and teachers in Baltimore also feared that transiency and truancy would lead to a group far behind their peers, and unprepared for the future direction of industry. Unlike their parents, there would be no unskilled jobs left in the urban economy for the migrants or their children. "These rural migrants come seeking employment. They are predominantly unskilled workers and the need for unskilled workers is decreasing all the time. Education is the only solution. Something must be done now, because in ten years there will be little need for unskilled workers."[22]

In Uptown poor southern migrants shared their schools with students from some affluent families whose homes were located near Lake Michigan. The parents of these wealthy students felt that migrant children had an adverse social effect on their children, as well as the entire community. Albert Votaw, of the Uptown Chicago Commission, proposed solutions to the problem. His idea called for separating the children into ungraded classes to solve the problem of students who were not ready for their grade levels.[23] He also sought to form a committee of civic leaders and educators to study the entire problem of transiency in the Stewart, Stockton, and Goudy elementary schools.[24] Behind the concern for migrant children Votaw and the Uptown Chicago Commission had a concern with declining property values. He feared that affluent residents alarmed at the decline in the neighborhood and schools would pull out of the area. The assumption that segregating them would somehow alleviate their maladjustment and transiency was a superficial, quick-fix solution at classroom management. In reality this was an attempt to appease wealthier citizens with children in the same schools. There is no indication that it would work to solve transiency or increase retention, which were the causes of the education problems in Uptown. The Sheriden Plaza meeting in 1957 concluded with the creation of the Kenmore-Uptown Center; a store front that provided instruction on practical matters such as using a gas stove and shopping, and activities for children. While the center was for all newcomers, it was primarily intended for southern white migrants since they were the largest group of newcomers in Uptown. It was widely believed at the time that southern migrants lacked basic ideas relating to living in urban areas. Most people who studied them felt that the solution to successful urban adaptation involved similar arrangements in other cities. Sociologist Roscoe Giffin, somewhat of an authority on southern migrants at the time, was involved in conducting workshops at Berea College for those working with urban migrants. Most of Giffin's advice centered on gaining an understanding of the worldview of migrants, and providing programs to ease the transition to urban life.[25] As for the Kenmore-Uptown Center, there is no evidence that southern migrants utilized it to any great extent. All indications are that it was short lived.[26] As will be seen, this model of essentially acculturating migrants would be repeated by many groups in Uptown.

The Chicago Southern Center (CSC) was the first organization in Uptown devoted solely to the southern white migrant. The CSC was an outgrowth of the Council of the Southern Mountains; a missionary organization based Berea,

Kentucky that grew out of the Southern Mountain Workers' Conference. By the late 1950s the Council of the Southern Mountains, under the direction of sociologist, Perley F. Ayer focused on cultural and religious traditions of Appalachia rather than the political battles engendered by industrialization of the region.[27] The CSM also sponsored annual workshops on Appalachian migrants in cities. These urban workshops were an effort to share information with those concerned with migration and settlement of urban Appalachians. Most of the activities of these workshops centered on education. Participants learned of migration trends, mountain culture, family structure, and problems that migrants may encounter in cities. Most of those who attended produced some sort of report, summarizing the content of the workshop. The reports were then made available to others working with migrants in cities. By and large the information was slanted heavily on mountain culture. As a result, it may not have pertained to those coming from other parts of the South. Nevertheless, it was probably the only coherent source of accurate knowledge that these urbanites received about migrants in their cities.

The Chicago Southern Center got its start after Fred Lickerman of the Boys Clubs of America and William Meyers of Combined Insurance Company in Uptown attended an urban workshop in 1962. Both men returned from the workshop in Berea highly concerned that the flow of migrants would increase and aggravate the problems of adjustment that migrants were experiencing. With the Kenmore-Uptown Center closed, Meyers and Lickerman appealed to Meyers' boss, W. Clement Stone, an eccentric philanthropist and owner of Combined Insurance in Uptown, to sponsor a center for migrants in Uptown. Stone, who in some way funded most private organizations in Uptown, had built his fortune by insurance. He made cold calling an art, and in the process, perfected his sales strategies into a philosophy of success that he called Positive Mental Attitude (PMA). He wrote two books on the subject and was a strong believer in self-help through internal motivation. In a speech at the Chicago Southern Center, Stone reviewed his philosophy:

> I pointed out the essence of success in any given activity comprises three principles, Inspiration to Action - How you get a person to get into action so that in a given environment you do what is right? The second is Know How and third, Activity Knowledge. If you go fishing you give the fish what the fish wants. We have to find out what they [southern migrants] want, to be assured with the motivational factor. Thereby the individual gets to know that as a person he is important that he has a conscious and a sub-conscious mind. And through his mind he can direct his thoughts and he can control his emotions and thus ordain his destiny.[28]

Stone believed that the social problems of the migrants in Uptown could be solved through his PMA principles. He felt that their problem was a lack of motivation inherent in southern culture. Meyers and Lickerman knew that Stone would grant their request if it promoted his PMA philosophy. In their proposal they stressed that the funds would be to establish a center to help migrants adjust to urban life and especially aid children with health, education through the Boys Clubs and other agencies. However, they hoped to stop migrant flow to Uptown as well. Both men saw a link between neighborhood instability, and the southern migrant. They were concerned that if trends continued the worst was yet to hit Chicago. One passage contained in the request conveyed particular urgency. "Unless something is done now to help the people of the hills to stay in their native areas—and to elevate themselves there—Chicago is in for many more social problems that it now has to endure."[29] Two days later Stone came through with the $25,000 requested by Lickerman and Meyers. Stone wanted the money to be used for a revolving fund rather than operating expenses. He also wanted an organization that would attract industry to the South—an unfulfilled request. That same month Meyers and Lickerman met with Pearly F. Ayer, Executive Director of the Council of the Southern Mountains in Berea Kentucky to choose a staff for the Chicago office of the Council of the Southern Mountains (later known as the Chicago Southern Center). They set themselves the difficult task of locating what would amount to a Harvard hillbilly to direct the center. They wanted a man with industrial and business sense, a southern accent, and fund-raising ability. At the same time the center was supposed to help migrants adjust to city life. In spite of the Stone's aversion to making the Chicago Southern Center a social work agency, the board chose Dewey Wood, a former social worker who had extensive work with Appalachian migrants in Cincinnati. Wood had no past experience in business and was not from the South.

Wood located an office in the middle of Uptown. In October of 1963, Wood wrote to the board members advising them that the two-room space in a storefront in the 4600 block of North Kenmore Avenue was open. Clothing bins and a food pantry were located in one room and the director's desk in the other. The donated furniture was arranged informally to welcome migrants who were encouraged to visit even without problems.[30] Future plans called for a study center with classes in job hunting, quilting, and music. Wood also believed that it was necessary to establish a network of cooperation with other social agencies in Uptown. Wood, Lickerman and Meyer convened a meeting of community leaders in November of the same year. The aim of the meeting was to open up communication and establish a network with community workers, police and services available to migrants in Uptown. Participants focused on how to alleviate migrant social problems and looked to the Southern Center for guidance and understanding.

The CSC had problems almost immediately. The center was in the awkward position of answering to the parent organization in Berea, being influenced by board members in Chicago, while continually relying on Stone for financial support. Wood was pulled in three directions. From the beginning, financial problems and fund raising plagued the Chicago Southern Center. Moreover, Ayer and Wood locked horns. Both men had short fuses. Wood outraged Ayer with his cavalier attitude. In one memorandum, Ayer wrote that Wood was more concerned with his social image and the country club set than the mission of the center. Ayer was referring to the fact that Wood had asked Stone to pay for his country club dues. In addition, Wood had not been keeping appointments with local businessmen. Ayer worried that Wood was in over his head.[31] By June of 1964, Stone's $25,000 grant was almost gone, and Wood was showing signs of desperation. He had borrowed heavily from the grant to cover operating expenses of the office in Chicago. He was also using the seed money for general council purposes.[32] Wood left after exactly one year on the job citing a desire to return to the field of social work, and obtain an advanced academic degree. Others, however, believe that the strained relationship with Ayer was the reason that Wood left.[33]

Before leaving, Wood recommended his young assistant, Raleigh Campbell to replace him. Campbell, a native of Leslie, Kentucky, who had recently joined the staff, had been a student of Ayer's at Berea College. Campbell seemed perfect for the position, but Ayer preferred someone with more experience. He chose Harry Woodward for the position. Woodward, a South Carolinian, had extensive experience with southern migrants in the Lakeview community in Chicago. Woodward's high profile energy and enthusiasm were well known among public and private agencies. He had been in Chicago since 1958, and had written one of the most definitive reports on southern migrants in Chicago in 1961. He was familiar with city agencies, community groups, business leaders, and had developed an extensive network among them. Campbell would remain on as migration consultant.[34]

Between 1964 and 1966, Woodward and Campbell raised the visibility of the Chicago Southern Center. Both were southerners with diverse, yet complementary, skills. They were a good team. Woodward was the administrator and primary involved in fund raising. Campbell, the social worker, walked the streets and visited the homes of southern families. Campbell was able to forge important relationships in the southern community, and made headway in understanding the informal structure of the community. Campbell's rural Kentucky roots and easygoing demeanor won him support among southerners and city officials. Everyone liked him. Virginia Bowers recalled Campbell's laid-back down home style. "He'd come around to your house to see if you were doing okay, you know. If you had problems, he would help you with that."[35] When police were stymied with tight-mouthed southerners, they asked Campbell to find out what was going on. Few if any organizations could claim acceptance by southern families. Campbell bridged the gap between the southern families and a social organization. Woodward, in turn, lobbied business and the city for funds and recruited influential board members. The heavy social clout and visibility of W. Clement Stone gave Woodward important access to the elite in Chicago.[36]

The CSC emerged as the center of social and cultural activities that were distinctly southern. Because it was an extension of the Council of the Southern Mountains, many of the activities carried out by the Chicago Southern Center were aimed at reaffirming southern culture rather than taking political stances. Events such as hosting Harriet Arnow, author of *The Dollmaker*, about Appalachian migrants to Detroit were common. The warm ambience of the center stood in stark contrast with the unwelcome reception many migrants received in Chicago. Migrants were finally welcomed to some place on their own terms. Few could claim the achievements that Campbell made during his time at the CSC. He had elevated the Center as a home base for southern migrants. This was evident in a report that he compiled to Ayer. "The Spirit of the people is that they say that they feel at home at the center. One woman said that she had been living here for twelve years and she is just beginning to feel at home. The square dance last week had 250 people in attendance. One person said that she would be doing something like this at home."[37] Campbell had accomplished what no other center had in the past. He had succeeded in providing a semblance of home in Chicago. The cultural events such as square dancing, quilting, and guitar lessons provided a setting for social interaction. He believed that the CSC should encourage certain aspects of southern identity, while adopting survival strategies to adjust to urban life:

> Having a center where people could develop an identity. It was a place where they could hold on to parts of their culture which was positive and learn the skills to make it in the new culture. Once you get an identity and a stabilized platform, then you could deal with issues. My focus was on the people and their needs. . .to make them feel welcome, a place that they owned.[38]

Campbell envisioned a multipurpose center which would grow out of the needs of southern migrants in Uptown. He wanted to solicit their input. Campbell began visiting the homes of migrants informally to discuss their experience adjusting to life in Chicago. By January of 1965, Campbell was visiting ten families a week. Two functions developed from these visits: daily services and long-term programs. Daily services provided to migrants consisted of clothing, emergency loans, and a community food pantry. Help was available with routine tasks such as, filling out job applications, obtaining birth certificates from back home, and locating apartments.[39] There were also long-term programs held at the CSC. Although some (guitar lessons, quilting, and sewing) were culturally based, the Center also sponsored alcoholics anonymous, employment services, and motivational seminars. W. Clement Stone often conducted seminars personally. Stone believed that his Positive Mental Attitude would lift migrants out of poverty much like it had done for him. Campbell was achieving a great deal of success. A year later, in a 1966 board meeting, he described a typical day at the Center. Campbell was very proud of his work. He remained optimistic about what the CSC had done for southern migrants. While not accomplishing all he had set out to do, he was confident that the CSC had done what few mainstream organizations had done previously for southern migrants.

> On an average day, 183 persons ranging from infancy to the seventies visit the Center to ask for help or search for a feeling of belonging at the Center. Each day about twenty-three individuals will come to the Center asking for employment or counseling. The director then calls factories in the area and arranges for job interviews. Thirty-eight women will enter the Center on an average day to participate in a home planning course centered around a sewing Circle. Forty individuals will participate in the Alcoholic Anonymous programs which are conducted by volunteers. The additional eighty-two will come seeking emergency rations or other help.[40]

Between its inception in November of 1963 and December 31, 1964, the center had served nearly 200 different families and 443 children. Eighty five percent of the families had five or fewer children. The median number of children per family was two. Eighty percent of the clients were male-headed households.[41] By 1966 the center was serving 250 people a month. A year later, over a thousand a month were using the center.[42] Part of the success was the bottom-up approach developed by Campbell, replicated unsuccessfully by the Urban Progress Center and other agencies throughout the decade. The CSC was a home away from home and a psychological cushion of support. Campbell hoped to achieve the mission of the CSM and the goals set out early by Meyers with this mix of cultural and practical services.[43] Members of the Chicago Southern Center marked the end of 1965 with hope and a feeling of accomplishment. A letter written to Ayer by Campbell expresses his emotional dedication, commitment and the hope southern migrants felt: "In this type of work, we struggle from day to day never really knowing if we had made an impression on others' lives, but we feel for once the Council can see some of the changes that we have wanted to see. Many of our Southern people in Chicago have faith in the future."[44]

One goal of the center was to cultivate a more favorable public perception of southern migrants. William Meyers carried out a one man campaign to improve the public perception of the migrant. His tireless work for the center was immeasurable. He was a wily public relations professional. He successfully lobbied the media for favorable portraits of southerners. In his words, he concentrated on "revamping the image of our migrant brethren." He convinced a popular radio station, WBBM to add a program about migrants in Chicago and the Southern Center.[45] He spoke to board members and industry leaders about changing the image from "poverty and sloth" to one of an "upright stalwart citizen." This would be accomplished through "public relations, publicity, and propaganda." Meyers viewed this as indispensable in the process of urban adaptation and acceptance by Chicagoans. In his eyes the southerner had been maligned by media stereotypes. It was the mission of the Chicago Southern Center to rectify this public misconception.[46] Meyer was able to influence media coverage of southern whites and the CSC. The focus of articles changed from reporting migrant criminality to highlighting their hopeful expectations. The knife wielding hillbillies became broom-pushing humble proletarians.[47] The articles credited the CSC with reducing the crime rate, finding employment for migrants, and fostering low rates of public aid. Officials in Uptown proclaimed that southern migrants were finally adjusting to life in Chicago. Some articles featured success stories of migrants who had made it in the North. Instead of the knife-wielding criminal, the migrant was an honest family man struggling to make ends meet on meager wages. Instead of spending his money on liquor, sex and cars, the Chicago migrant bought a hundred-pound sack of potatoes to feed his family. He'd lost his desire for bars, and his penchant for fighting.[48] Although this was highly unlikely, it was important for the public to have more positive perceptions about southern whites.

Newspapers which had previously published scathing articles on southern migrants pictured Campbell standing casually in the doorway of the CSC, and wrote about it as a beacon of hope for the migrant family.[49] As missionaries had gone into Appalachia, urban missionaries from the wealthy suburbs descended into Uptown to save the migrants. Upper middle class honor students tutored migrant children. The newspapers never completely shed the negative stereotypes. Although more favorable, the coverage contained a patronizing tone.[50] Nevertheless, the center was filling a niche in the community. Campbell was achieving his goal. Southerners were using the CSC as their own. They were coming in to participate in the activities and programs.

By 1969, the Center had interviewed over 7,000 clients, served over 34,000 migrants, sold over 200,000 items of clothing, and 12,557 food items. By that time only 17 percent of the clients had been to the center previously. For Campbell, this proved the effectiveness of his approach. The center was a source of motivation for migrants rather than a source of dependence. It was a hand up and out of poverty. This met with the organizational goals and philosophical mission of Stone's Positive Mental Attitude.[51] Stone's involvement added clout and legitimacy to the center and gave it a much higher profile that it would have had otherwise. It allowed Woodward and others to recruit prominent community leaders to serve on the Board of the Chicago Southern Center. It gave Woodward access to potential donors. Finally, Meyers' public relations machine provided a steady flow of media coverage. This quelled groups like the Uptown Chicago Commission, and other civic groups who had earlier feared a total cave-in of property values.

The board members of the Chicago Southern Center developed a network of cooperation with other city agencies. The board was composed of prominent members of the community, including members of the Mayor's Commission on Youth Welfare, police officials, representatives from the Uptown Chamber of Commerce, district superintendents of schools, social workers, and academics. At times, meetings resembled mini-workshops similar to those taking place at the

Council of the Southern Mountains in Berea. From these meetings, members of community agencies developed strategies, avoided duplication of services, made referrals. They coordinated efforts and learned ways to entice migrants to use their services.

One direct outgrowth of this inter-agency cooperation was the involvement of the Uptown Boys Club with migrant children. In addition to regular recreational activities, the Boys Club sponsored summer camps, dental care, baths, and free physical exams.[52] Ideas for medical programs also emerged from assessing the needs of the neighborhood children. Volunteer physicians from nearby Weiss Memorial Hospital gave every member of the Boys Club a physical, and vision and dental exams.[53] The physical was conducted in a military format with large groups of boys in a gym. Tom Moore was an enthusiastic director of the Boys Clubs during this time. In an interview, he discussed the origins of the exams for the children.

> We met a man who was head of medical education at Weiss. He said, 'I'd be happy to work with you. I will bring the interns over two or three times a year and we'll do a physical.' It was like an army physical. We stripped the kids down in a gym and did the whole thing. Then Northwestern agreed to set up a dentist in the club to offer dental services to the kids. Eventually we had vision screening there. Exams were recorded on the back of the club cards. When a kid came in we looked on the back of his card to check that he had been examined. If not he was sent to the exam. If a principal called and a kid came to school dirty, we'd go get them give them a shower and take them back to school.[54]

Concern for health was especially high after the Tuberculosis institute of Chicago and Cook County reported that Uptown led the city in the disease. The area had the highest number of deaths from the illness in 1959.[55] This was especially important during the diphtheria panic in Uptown. In 1962, Southerners were blamed for bringing the illness to Chicago from Alabama. These programs helped quell the fear of disease ridden migrants, while at the same time served the interests of public health.

The Uptown Boys Club had outgrown its capacity as thousands of southern children swelled the ranks of its membership. At one point the club with a capacity of 200 claimed over 900 members and was operating out of a former three-room laundry.[56] W. Clement Stone, now chairman of the Chicago Boys Clubs, financed part of the construction of the new $1 million Boys Club on Sheriden Avenue named after Robert R. McCormick. Among those pictured at the opening of the new Uptown Boys Club in 1957 were, Phil Hampton, of the McCormick charitable trust, W. Clement Stone, and a stern-looking Mayor Daley.[57] With over 4,000 members, the McCormick club became the largest club in the system and even attracted celebrities. On one occasion, John Wayne showed up for a visit and was pictured in the Uptown News holding a young southern boy in his arms.[58]

The Boys Club worked closely educating children. After school tutoring programs were set up in conjunction with elementary schools in the area. They hired teachers from the school in the summer. Former director Tom Moore also used the club to mediate problems children had in an unofficial manner. Meeting between parents, police, principals, and club officials were a regular part of community outreach. This relieved the pressure of going to a meeting in an official location such as a police station.[59] By becoming involved in community problems, the Boys Club gained a great degree of trust from the migrant children. Children turned to club when there was no where else to go. While their parents may have used the Chicago Southern Center, their children were spent their time at the Boys Club. Again Tom Moore commented that, "the southern white kids loved it. It was like a family, and they were very clannish and family oriented. So whenever anything went wrong, if they were running away from home, they'd come and tell you. If they were having problems in school and didn't know where to go they'd come and tell you."[60]

Former director of the club, Lickerman elaborated on the reason for the club's attraction to southern migrants. He believed that southern migrants had gained a sense of attachment to their neighborhood. In an interview he said "they [southern migrants] felt comfortable at the Boys Club because their numbers were so large, so it was like their club. It belonged to them."[61] Uptown was emerging as home for these young migrants. However, it was only through active outreach that this was accomplished. Lickerman and Moore believed in reaching out because many had no idea that the club existed. Lickerman made extensive community contacts when he first arrived in Uptown. Much like the Southern Center's Raleigh Campbell had done, Lickerman had to walk the streets to generate interest and attention for the Boys Club in Uptown. He expressed pride in his accomplishment. "When I came in 1956 with a three-room operation, to really offer a meaningful services, you had to run a decentralized program. So you had to get into the churches, you had to get into the schools. So you were out. You weren't in a building."[62] Through contact with the community, Lickerman and Moore developed services tailored to the needs of the migrants which contributed to the success of the Boys Clubs in Uptown during the 1960s.

An order of nuns also focused their efforts at aiding migrants in a unique way. The Appalachian Study Center (ASC) founded in 1964 had many similarities to the Chicago Southern Center. Located just three blocks south of the Chicago Southern Center on Kenmore Avenue, the ASC was run by The Glenmary Sisters. This Catholic religious order was best known for their efforts in Appalachia. Though it is highly unlikely that many of these migrants were Catholic, the ASC sisters had some success. Similar to the Southern Center, their approach emphasized home visits. Instead of relying on clients to walk in to their offices for services, the Glenmary Sisters became part of the neighborhood. Unlike the Southern Center, Appalachian Center focused only on the 4300 Block of Kenmore Avenue. This block contained the largest concentration of southern whites in Uptown. It was characterized by large multi-family flats containing hundreds of southern families. It was in this neighborhood that photographers captured half-clothed children playing under the shadow of the elevated trains and junk cars. Little information survives on their activities other than several memos and one report clarifying their activities and research in 1965. While not detailing or quantifying results, the documents provide a colorful overview of the philosophical underpinnings and daily activities of the ASC. The ASC was engaged in three broad areas of work, research, action, and training. They viewed their mission as a program of community development from the ground up based on the needs of the migrants. Their plans were ambitious. In addition to undertaking the task of understanding the values and needs of the Southern people, their research endeavored to comprehend the "effects of migration on the family structure."[63] Primary among their efforts was meeting the immediate needs of the migrants during their first two weeks in Chicago. Similar to the CSC, they helped migrants find jobs, housing, and emergency loans. The Glenmary sisters helped southern whites organize holiday festivals, block club meetings, music lessons, and emergency food distribution. Finally, the ASC programs concentrated on integrating migrants into the larger community and steering them to the department of public aid, the Chicago Southern Center and public schools. Again their success lay in the approach the sisters used. Experience in more isolated parts of Appalachia taught them to go out to the people. They brought this strategy to Chicago and utilized it in an urban setting.

In the course of operating, the Chicago Southern Center evolved away from the original intent of its founders. Rather than stemming the flow of migrants as originally envisioned by Stone, Meyers, and Lickerman, the Southern Center and groups like the Glenmary Sisters encouraged migration by providing a haven for the migrants, and recreating the familiar elements of home, and helping them locate employment. This was not unlike other ethnic-based groups in history. Few differences existed between the CSC and the Migration Division for Puerto Ricans in New York, for example. In fact, the head of that organization, Clarence Senior, consulted regularly with the Council of the Southern Mountains, and participated in their workshops on urban adjustment.[64] The importance of the Chicago Southern Center should not be underestimated. Although Stone's intent to attract industry to the South was never attained, the CSC was a major unifying force for the southern migrant community in Uptown. It provided cohesion to a community which had become alienated from mainstream institutions and social welfare agencies. By promoting southern identity as something positive, the CSC instilled pride in a group shunned by many in Chicago. Although not all migrants were from Appalachia, the focus on common southern origins allowed all southern migrants some measure of identity and solidarity. The CSC altered public opinion and reduced stereotypes about southern migrants by demonstrating that they wanted to become productive members of society rather than receiving welfare.

Campbell knew that he would have to go into the neighborhoods and talk to southerners. His aim was to prove that the Chicago Southern Center was part of the community. Campbell was legitimate. He was southern. He was not condescending. This was essential to being accepted by the southern migrants. By networking with other social agencies in Uptown, the CSC opened the door for organizations like the Boys Clubs and the Glenmary Sisters. These organizations were effective and accepted largely due to grassroots efforts of Campbell. Southern migrants were gradually becoming a part of the community. The public support of W. Clement Stone added additional legitimacy to the CSC for the more affluent in Chicago. Without the CSC, it is doubtful that later efforts by JOIN to organize migrants into an action coalition would have succeeded so quickly. More importantly, the CSC was the first organization to approach migrants as southerners with a common identity.

Economic problems and dilapidated housing continued to affect southern migrants, however. These were issues that the Chicago Southern Center would not address because of their mission. The CSC avoided any controversial issues. As a result, the CSC did not reach a certain impoverished segment of the migrant population in Uptown. Although Uptown was slated to receive large amounts of War on Poverty money, it did little to alleviate the source of the economic woes, or pitiful housing conditions. Another organization emerged to represent southern whites in Uptown. Similar to Raleigh Campbell these student activists relied on organizing migrants at the grassroots level. Unlike the CSC, which sought to integrate migrants into traditional social institutions, the Students for a Democratic Society's program Jobs or Income Now (JOIN) focused on challenging mainstream social institutions. It linked the plight of southern migrants to the worldwide struggle against capitalism. In a political environment that was increasingly defined along interests of race, Uptown was a perfect staging ground. There were large numbers of poor whites, deteriorated housing, and high unemployment.

Notes

1. "Poor People's Power in Uptown," *Chicago Tribune Magazine*, 28 September 1968, 46–50(N).
2. "Poor People's Power in Uptown."
3. *New York Times*, 31 August 1963.
4. "What is a Hillbilly?" *Hazard Herald*, 28 February 1963.
5. "Southern Whites Too Proud to Ask for Help Here." *Chicago Daily News*, 13 August 1959, 1(N)."Appalachian Migrants Fail to Benefit from Antipoverty Drive, " *Wall Street Journal*, 30 September 1965.
6. David E. Whisnet, *Modernizing the Mountaineer: People, Planning and Power in Appalachia* (Boone, North Carolina: Appalachian Consortium Press, 1980), 19–23
7. Personal interview by the author with Tom Moore, former program director for the Robert R. McCormick Boys Club, 20 April 1994.

8. "Ask Transient Center for Uptown Students," *Edgewater-Uptown News*, 31 December 1957, 1(N).

9. Internal communication from Fred Lickerman and Bill Meyers to W. Clement Stone, March 11, 1963, Papers of the Council of the Southern Mountains, Southern Appalachian Archives, Box 74.

10. " T.B. Still a Menace: Tests Indicate 1606 Cases." *Edgewater- Uptown News*, 26 March 1957, 1(N). "Uptown Leads Area in T.B. Cases," *Edgewater-Uptown News*, 23 August 1960, 1(N). "Uptown's Pain of Poverty Eases," *Chicago Daily News*, 5 March 1966.

11. "A Summary of the Work of the Migration Services Department, Mayors Committee on New Residents, January 1957–1959," Chicago Commission on Human Relations, March 1959.

12. Bert Schloss, " The Uptown Community and the Southern White In-Migrant." (Chicago: Chicago Commission on Human Relations, 1957).

13. "Poor People's Power in Uptown, 47.

14. Milton Gordon, *Assimilation in American Life: The Role of Race, Religion and National Origins* (New York: Oxford University Press, 1964).

15. "Uptown Adopts Five-Point Program for New Residents," *Edgewater Uptown News*, July 2, 1957, 1(N).

16. "The Uptown Area and the Southern In-Migrant," 11.

17. "Transient School Pupils," *Uptown Edgewater News*, 6 January 1957, 4 (N).

18. National Council of Jewish Women. "The Unaccepted Baltimoreans: A Report on the White Southern Rural Migrants" (May 1961), 6

19. "A Report on the Opening of the Chicago Office of the Council of the Southern Mountains." (Unpublished report, November 1963) Southern Appalachian Archives.

20. Ora Spaid, "Southerners Shuttle North, Back,"*Louisville Courier-Journal*, 21 October 1959,6 (N).

21. "The Unaccepted Baltimoreans."

22. "The Unaccepted Baltimoreans."

23. "Ask Transient Center for Uptown Students."

24. "Uptown Adopts Five Point Program for New Residents."

25. Roscoe Giffin, "Newcomers from the Southern Mountains," *Selected Papers, Institute on Cultural Patterns of Newcomers* (Welfare Council of Metropolitan Chicago, October 1957): 15–40.

26. "New Families Learn to Live 'The Chicago Way' at Center," *Edgewater-Uptown News*, 30 April 1957, 1(N).

27. David E. Whisnant, *Modernizing the Mountaineer: People, Planning and Power in Appalachia*. (Boone: Appalachian Consortium Press, 1980), 3–42.

28. This was an excerpt from speech was given at the Chicago Southern Center on January 16, 1964. Southern Appalachian Archives, Box 284-3.

29. Internal correspondence from Fred Lickerman and William Meyers to W. Clement Stone, March 11, 1963. Council of the Southern Mountains records, Southern Appalachian Archives.

30. "News From Chicago Office." Memorandum sent to the Board Members of the Council of the Southern Mountains in Berea Kentucky from Dewy Wood on February 17, 1964. Southern Appalachian Archives, Box 102-13.

31.Correspondence from Perly F. Ayer to Dewey Wood. June 17, 1964. Council of the Southern Mountains Collection. Southern Appalachian Archives, Box 102-13.

32. This was revealed at the minutes of a CSC meeting on June 10, 1964. Of the $25,000 initially provided by Stone, only $5,070.44 remained.

33.Correspondence to P.F. Ayer from Dewey Wood, dated July 31, 1964. Southern Appalachian Archives, Box 102-13. This second fact was discussed in a personal interview on August 4, 1995 with Raleigh Campbell, a staff member during the time.

34. From a Council of the Southern Mountains press release, dated 1964. Southern Appalachian Archives, Box 106-13.

35. Personal interview by the author with Virginia Bowers, 18 March 1994.

36. Personal interview by the author with Raleigh Campbell interview, 4 August 1994.

37. Minutes from and executive meeting of the Chicago Center, on March 20, 1966. Southern Appalachian Archives. Box 283-10.

38. Campbell interview.

39. Minutes of a board meeting of the Chicago Southern Center, May 31, 1966. Southern Appalachian Archives, Box 283-10.

40. These comments and the functions of the Center were described in a program report from the Chicago branch of the Council of the Southern Mountains in January 1965. Southern Appalachian Archives, Box 284-3.

41. "Program Report." Council of Southern Mountains, January 1965, Southern Appalachian Archives, Box 284-3.

42. "Directors Report." Chicago Southern Center, March 1967. Southern Appalachian Archives, Box 284-1.

43. One of Meyers goals in his proposal letter to Stone in 1963 was to reduce the tendency to commute between home and Chicago. By stabilizing the migrants their burden to the Uptown community would lessen. Because no data exists on return migration it is unclear if this goal was full realized.

44. Correspondence from Raleigh to Perley F. Ayer, dated December 16, 1965. Southern Appalachian Archives, Box 283-8.

45.Correspondence from William H. Meyers to Karl D. Bays, dated February 2, 1965. Southern Appalachian Archives, Box 283-8.

46. Personal correspondence from William Meyers to Karl D. Bays, dated March 23, 1965. Examples of this are contained in Meyer's correspondence to the author, Harriet Arnow, on April 21, 1965. Southern Appalachian Archives, Box 283-8.

47. "Chicago Migrants Finding Hope," *New York Times*, 27 March 1966, 84(N).

48. "Man Can Make it Up Here if He Really Tries," *National Observer* (partial date, 1966) Southern Appalachian Archives, Box 294-1.

49. "Mountain Folks Learn Ways of Urban Life." *Chicago Tribune*, 28 November 1965.

50. "Her Real Education: Tutoring Migrants." *Chicago Daily News*, 5 June 1965.

51. Taken from letter written by Donald Tuomi, President of the Chicago Southern Center Board for a 1969 fund-raising campaign. Southern Appalachian Archives, Box 284-2.

52. Untitled photograph, *Edgewater-Uptown News*, 17 May 1960. Subsequently confirmed in a personal interview with Tom Moore, former director of the Uptown Boys Club on 20 April 1994.

53. "Boys Club Marks First Year By Inviting All Boys This Week. " *Edgewater-Uptown News*, 11 April 1961, 1 (N).

54. Tom Moore interview.

55. "Uptown Leads Area in T.B. Cases." *Edgewater-Uptown News*, 23 August 1960, 1(N).

56. "Start Drive for New Boys Club," *Edgewater-Uptown News*, 1 July 1952, 1(N).

57. Untitled photograph, *Edgewater-Uptown News*, 12 April 1960.

58. *Edgewater-Uptown News*, 10 November 1960.

59. Tom Moore interview.

60. Tom Moore interview

61. Personal interview by the author with Fred Lickerman, 5 April 1994.

62. Lickerman interview.

63. This was an untitled document about the Appalachian Study Center in the author's possession. It was obtained by writing to the Glenmary Sisters in Smithland, Ky.

64. For the Puerto Rican Example see Virginia Sánchez Korral, *From Colonia to Community: The History of Puerto Ricans in New York City* (Berkley: University of California Press, 1983). Senior's participation in the workshops was noted in a participant's report in 1959. Southern Appalachian Archives, Box 278-1.

Chapter 6

Southern Unity and Social Protest in Uptown

We were doing pretty bad until we met up with JOIN. The way I met up with JOIN was I noticed a one-arm guy named Ras, he and another guy was drunk. Had on a JOIN button. I never did go to the meetings until a long time after that. And that's when JOIN helped me out. When I had that fire at 1047 West Buena, I got over three hundred dollars in General Assistance. If it wasn't for JOIN, I guess we wouldn't have it now.[1]

They [JOIN] agitate rather than seeking to serve the people. When they have nothing to agitate about they will be out of business.[2]

Though seemingly at odds, these two quotes above accurately depicted the scene in Uptown by the middle sixties. Sarah Dotson's often-stated saying , "if you can't get a job in Chicago you can't get a job anywhere" began to wear thin. Southerners who arrived from the South were not finding work as well as they were ten years earlier. The tactics of protest that the student organizers involved in JOIN (Jobs or Income Now) used were provocative, and rarely seen on the grassroots level in Uptown. While organizations like the Chicago Southern Center cultivated southern pride, JOIN took this one step further and added a dimension of social protest. While the CSC focused on families and more traditional means of urban integration such as job placement, counseling and cultural activities, JOIN organized migrants to fight for better housing, welfare rights, and protest against police brutality. This chapter argues that JOIN, a program initiated by student activists from the SDS (Students for a Democratic Society), mobilized a poorer segment of southern whites in Uptown against encroachment by developers, poverty and police brutality. JOIN emphasized community power and unity of the poor. Social protest was a new means to resist police brutality and urban renewal and to improve their living conditions. The success of JOIN and the social activism of southern migrants was facilitated by the unity they had developed previously, by crowded conditions, and by events taking place in Uptown. The fledgling southern identity gained by affiliation with the Chicago Southern Center gave JOIN a base from which to appeal to southern migrants. Although the JOIN office opened a year after the Chicago Southern Center, their aims were very different. Part of this had to do with their origins and financial backing. The CSC emerged out of a desire to assimilate southerners by easing the rural to urban transition, and providing them with the means to adapt to life in Chicago. At the same time, an effort was made to provide those working with migrants the tools to understand them through the urban workshops held in Berea, Kentucky. When Campbell went into blocks inhabited by southern whites and asked them what they needed, he meant what they needed to adapt socially and economically. The CSC's parent organization, the Council of the Southern Mountain avoided political causes. As a result the CSC avoided political causes. This tendency to avoid controversy was reinforced because funding was derived from conservative businessmen like W. Clement Stone. Although Campbell may have sympathized with southern whites experiencing unnecessary violence from police, his response would not have involved picketing the police precinct. When southerners complained about the paucity of jobs, or the lack of opportunity, the CSC was likely to respond with job training or by promoting more positive images of southern whites. Because JOIN was a product of the SDS, their view of these issues was very different. Joblessness, police brutality, and, inadequate housing, were logical outcomes of a manifestly unjust economic system. The solution therefore did not involve job training, cooperation with police, or a quilting class. In Uptown it involved confronting these issues through more direct means such as picketing and rent strikes. On a national level the SDS embraced fundamental change in the American economic and political structure.[3]

Some southern white migrants remained caught in the cycle of unstable work, inadequate wages, and unemployment. Temporary work and daily pay made obtaining stable employment difficult.[4] Moreover, traditional industrial work which paid well, had begun a descent that would remain unabated. In an odd way, Stone's desire to attract industry to the South was happening. Throughout the twentieth century, heavy industry left rustbelt cities of the Midwest for Sunbelt cities in the South. As a result, the dream of financial stability rarely became a reality. West Virginia migrant, James Lambert recalled that men "could earn good money in steel, but they kept getting laid off." His comments testify to the larger economic changes affecting Chicago and other northern cities during the 1960s which would accelerate in the 1970s. Between 1948 and 1977 Chicago lost over 300,000 manufacturing jobs. Similar losses were recorded in the wholesale and retail sectors. During this period, the only job growth occurred in selected services requiring much more education than most migrants possessed, or low paying work in the service sector.[5] A skills mismatch was occurring in Chicago and other Midwestern cities. Southern migrants with limited education and menial skills were arriving in cities that were beginning to experience unprecedented job losses in employment sectors for which they were most qualified.

Well-paying work was episodic at best. Temporary agencies reigned in Uptown. Unemployed southern migrants and a slowly increasingly population of deinstitutionalized mentally ill found themselves together in the neighborhood. Many of the migrants were falling into a daily-pay trap. Those who were opposed to the temporary agencies argued that they were perpetuating a cycle of dependency. The scenario was familiar to many migrants and observers. After coming to Chicago, some found that their educational level, accent, and appearance narrowed job prospects considerably. However, the numerous day-labor operations in Uptown hired these men. The low pay and the finder's fee severely reduced the net pay. By 1968, some migrants took home as little as $45 a week. Out of that $28 went for housing in one of the many furnished rooms or apartments in Uptown. Moreover, these positions carried no benefits such as health care for the children of migrants. A social services administrator in Chicago commented on the situation that "they [daily pay agencies] were getting $8.00 an hour for the guys and giving them $2.50, and the only place that you could cash your check is the neighborhood bar. It was a whole pattern and people got trapped in that life cycle."[6] This cycle not only encouraged dependency, but also prevented any return back home. Migrant and social activist, Chuck Geary commented on this dream of returning saying that "they [southern whites] ain't going back. That's just what some folks like to think. When a family disappears, it's because somebody sold them a TV they can't pay for, or they ain't got the rent."[7] Unable to find work, many southern white men drank. Loitering and fighting became common. Chronic unemployment undermined the traditional role of the male as breadwinner further eroding traditional family organization. Returning home was not an option. Many migrants felt cheated because they had traded family and kin ties at home for poverty in Chicago.

The southern white population had swelled and the shrinking social and economic structure could not absorb them. This aggravated and intensified community and police relations as more southern whites remained under-employed in Uptown. Apparently, the Chicago Southern Center had failed to reach the poorest segment of the southern whites in Uptown. The cauldron was simmering. Poverty, and unemployment were signs of an economy that was beginning to lose entry level industrial jobs. This problem not limited to southern whites in Uptown. Black southerners who migrated to Chicago to escape social and political oppression originally found employment in heavy industry. Immigration restrictions in the midst of World War I created a demanded for unskilled labor. As this demand increased during the War, labor recruiters fanned in the South offering blacks work in steel, railroads and auto industry. Although racism relegated blacks to substandard socio-economic status and second-class citizenship in the North, many had made significant gains.[8] The postwar World War II migration of blacks to Chicago had not paid off as well. On the south and west sides of Chicago, thousands of blacks from the South were unemployed and receiving public assistance by 1966.[9] Poverty was a national concern being voiced by prominent social scientists and policy makers. Michael Harrington's, *The Other America* awakened the national consciousness to the ravages of poverty in rural Appalachia and central cities.[10] The economic largess that had lifted other urban ethnic groups up and out to the suburbs was diminishing.

White poverty was concentrated in Uptown. A survey conducted in Uptown revealed an unemployment rate over 27 percent among those seeking work in 1966. When those who stopped looking for work were included, the unemployment rate rose to over 47 percent the majority of which were southern white migrants. These staggering figures did not include house wives and students. Seen another way, only

39.5 percent of the respondents were working full-time. Among those working, a substantial percentage had experienced long-term unemployment the previous year. This widespread joblessness was not related to length of time in Chicago. Only 5.3 percent of those interviewed had been in Chicago less than a year.[11] The loss of jobs in Chicago was apparent. Southern migrants in Uptown exceeded the number of stable jobs available.

Nationally, the social climate had changed by the mid-1960s. Urban issues were pushed to the forefront of national concern. The country was at war with an elusive enemy in Vietnam. Student activists on campuses were protesting the U.S. involvement in Southeast Asia. Groups like the weathermen and, black panthers struck fear in many middle-class Americans. Five summers of urban rioting had focused the nation's attention on growing racial unrest, forcing President Johnson to Issue Executive Order No. 11365 creating a National Advisory Commission on Civil Disorders. The "Kerner" Commission was tasked with determining causes and solutions for such urban disorders.[12] At the same time, the Civil Rights Movement challenged Washington to live up to core values and language of the Founding Fathers. Egalitarian rhetoric from Mao and Lenin picked open a wound by insisting that the future lay in annihilating class distinctions. It was from this new culture of protest that organizations like the SDS (Students for a Democratic Society) and its off shoot JOIN opened the Join Community Union office in the heart of the southern white neighborhood near the corner of Winthrop and Ainslie in January of 1964. The words of one biographer of JOIN tell of their intent upon opening the office. "We [members of JOIN] would offer ourselves to the people around JOIN, offer them a medium for their free expression—a book and amplification system, a chance to cast their light up from the bottom of this society with a special illumination that comes only from victims."[13] Victimization became the major lens though which southern whites would view themselves. Like other groups during this era of Civil Rights, their claim on the American Dream emanated from the belief of equality of opportunity. Their mean of achieving this would be social protest. In this case, they took their pleas to local institutions.

One of JOIN's first targets was the appalling housing that southern whites occupied. Housing had always been on the minds of the residents of Uptown. Initially the area offered affluent Chicagoans an escape from the densely populated inner city. Uptown flourished as an entertainment and retail district throughout the 1920s which spurred development. Residential hotels were constructed for single residents who could afford it, and large apartment buildings went up for families. Shortages of rental property had plagued the area since World War II when housing was needed to accommodate a steady influx of new residents. A steady and profitable process of converting larger apartments to smaller units began. More people chose the expanding suburbs over urban living throughout the 1950s. The aging housing and simultaneous decline of Uptown as an entertainment and retail district, left the area ripe for illegal and quick conversions. Following the exit of the middle-class residents, southern whites flooded the area seeking inexpensive housing. By the middle of 1960, much of the rental property in Uptown was in substandard condition, and woefully inadequate for habitation. Cheap or illegal conversions had left much of the many apartments in dangerous or in poor shape. Children often played in filthy rat-infested alleys. Well into the sixties, entire buildings were found illegal by inspectors. Unsafe porches and crash panel doors, and leaky roofs were only a part of the situation.[14] Rats, roaches, uncollected trash, and unsafe electrical outlets were reported by tenants. Lead poisoning was rampant. The average rent, however, continued to increase.[15]

The activists in JOIN encouraged southern whites to take to the streets and protest their living conditions. They used direct and brash confrontation to accomplish their goals. They used rent strikes, and instructed tenants to send their rent directly to Mayor Daley.[16] As Meyers had done with the Chicago Southern Center, they mobilized media coverage to work on their behalf. One particularly impressive picture showed three generations of men displaying three freshly killed rats in their living room. The landlord had cut off their electricity after falling behind on their rent allowing the rats free at night. The tenant had to stay up all night with an air rifle "to protect his children."[17] JOIN turned the tables on Uptown slumlords. They reminded tenants that it was the responsibility of owners to maintain safe buildings. They pointed out the city's lack of code enforcement and passivity regarding these deleterious conditions. Almost immediately JOIN won substantial concessions from Uptown landlords. Their overt tactics attracted the attention of the media and city hall to the deplorable conditions southern white migrants endured in their neighborhoods. Instead of waiting for the wheels of bureaucracy to turn, they picketed buildings. Rather than waiting for legal action to be taken, Rennie Davis and Patricia Deer met with owners and hammered out plans to meet tenants demands.[18] Tenants evicted in error were reinstated to their apartments. Letter writing campaigns were organized intended to call attention to the plight of residents. Direct action such as this eventually pressured the city. Many were surprised to see southern whites active in their own community. City Hall responded to their actions. History was made when housing inspectors were relocated to offices in Uptown to handle complaints of code violations.[19] There first victories energized the migrants, and they were an important element in JOIN gaining credibility among them.

JOIN was able to reach a smaller and impoverished segment of the southern white population. These migrants were disillusioned with the conditions in Uptown. Migration had not paid off as well for them. Housing was in poor shape. Their children ate lead paint peeling from dirty walls. Their landlords rarely maintained their buildings. The ally ways were full of uncollected garbage. Vermin roamed the alleys and apartments at night. Virginia Bowers, a southern white migrant and early member of JOIN, participated in many activities. She spoke to me from her apartment on Ainslie Street in Uptown some thirty years later. She remained connected to the plight of the poor. She was a lifelong activist. She recalled coaching her fellow migrants into active protest to alleviate their conditions and the costs associated with this. It seems unimaginable that tenants would have to resort to protest for such appalling conditions. It is also apparent that there were risks involved when residents took a stand against landlords.

> We had tenant strikes which I was involved in. I lost my first job as a manager in a building because I stuck up for a couple that had been bitten by a rat. The owner wanted me to lie about it. I told Tom [a housing inspector] that I couldn't lie to him. I was a mother myself, and I couldn't lie. The couple went to an organization called JOIN and complained about it to them. One of the main organizers came to my house and we set up a meeting. The landlord would not attend. After that we took him [the landlord] to court.[20]

Virginia's comments point to a central difference between JOIN and the Chicago Southern Center. Whereas the CSC encouraged assimilation and accommodation by steering migrants into to stable entry level jobs and affordable apartments, JOIN organized rent strikes, and lobbied for better welfare benefits. The CSC under the direction of Raleigh Campbell or any director would not resort to brash tactics such as suing a landlord. Using these methods JOIN was more effective in getting southern whites to take to the streets in protest. Moreover, as long as they saw results, southerners continued to support JOIN.

JOIN members were media savvy and did not shy away from controversy. They were vocal about the underbelly of urban renewal which meant mass displacement of southern whites from Uptown. Mass evictions would mean losing their power base as well. In 1967, they charged the urban renewal board, the Conservation Community Council (CCC) with being largely made up of the business-dominated Uptown Conservation Council (UCC) which did not represent the interests of the poor.[21] They convinced the southern whites that the UCC wanted to rid Uptown of the poor. Central to their message was the preservation of home from the forces of removal. This rhetoric echoed with southern migrants, many of whom had begin to establish roots in Uptown, and were unable to return to the South. Campaigns against urban renewal included a poster of a grandmother in a rocking chair with the caption "some people just don't take naturally to moving." Children carrying placards were often a part of demonstrations and marches. The efforts of JOIN were effective in redirecting blame and pointing the finger at landlords for maintaining the slum conditions that many southern whites lived in during the sixties. While the alderman campaigned for razing the eyesores in Uptown, Members of JOIN made it clear that there must be affordable replacement housing for southern whites. In doing so they racked up the ire of property and business owners, and reminded boosters that the hailed "upswing in Uptown" excluded the poor. The fell in step with much of the stated ideology of the SDS's "Port Huron Statement" and the student members of JOIN.

The police maintained a tight grip on the residents of Uptown. Anyone with a southern accent was likely to face police brutality and harassment. Because JOIN members were often students, they did not hesitate to provoke city officials or the police. In August of 1966, JOIN led 150 southerners on a march to the Foster Avenue police station demanding that one officer be transferred for malfeasance of duty.[22] Leading the march were numerous younger southern whites whose parents had migrated to Uptown. They had united against police abuse and had adopted the name, the Goodfellows. Patterned after the Puerto Rican, Young Lords, they had organized community patrols armed with notebooks to record abuses and badge numbers. Particularly menacing to southern white migrants was an Uptown cop with a history of abuse. Although many events precipitated the march, the flash point was sexual abuse by the police. A former member of JOIN recalled that it involved the rape of a young southern white woman by an officer stationed in Uptown.

> When I was managing the office of JOIN, I had a young girl come in there crying, and I asked her what's the matter. And she said that so and so policeman took her out to Foster Avenue Beach and she had to have sex with him. They couldn't do anything about it 'cause he was a policeman. So we had a big demonstration at the police department. We got down there and had eggs thrown at us tomatoes whatever. After that, they would not fire that policeman because he was too close to retirement.[23]

JOIN gained additional support the Sunday before the march when raging police arrested and openly clubbed a young southerner in front of a large crowd of onlookers. Amelia Jenkins witnessed the beating. She stated that, "he was already handcuffed. They [the police] had throwed him down. They hit him with their billy clubs and they was jabbin' him in the stomach. They hit him, all three cops, one, two, three, boom, boom, boom. They got him down and had his face pushed up against the curb, and handcuffed his feet together."[24] This event nearly erupted into a small riot when the crowd began to taunt the police. Fortunately for JOIN, it added urgency and intensity to the demonstration at the police station the following Tuesday. Police were well acquainted with JOIN and knew that they had encouraged migrants to protest police brutality. Such events also strengthened the unity of southern whites in Uptown. The Police raided JOIN headquarters and southern taverns in retaliation. JOIN, in turn, accused the police of planting illegal drugs and harassment.[25] With these tactics JOIN accomplished something that the CSC was unable to do. By challenging the police and holding them accountable, they instilled a spirit of rebellion among migrants. JOIN members stressed the prerogative of opposition. Southern whites developed an attachment to their neighborhoods because they had a stake in the events. The action of protesting inadvertently instilled, in southerners, a sense of ownership in their community. It initiated a wave of social protest that remains alive today in Uptown. Southern whites continue to be mistreated by the police and respond similarly. During the course of this research, a woman from Tennessee died in her apartment. When the police arrived, their actions were humiliating to observers and neighbors. Soon after this incident, there was a march through Uptown culminating in a demonstration against police mistreatment of the woman.[26]

During the sixties, it was clear to most people in Uptown that to be associated with JOIN brought police harassment. With Hoover's COINTELLPRO (Counter

Intelligence Program) in full swing FBI agents visited bars, and any organizations believed to be sympathetic to JOIN. By 1966 the SDS had 200,000 members nationwide and was targeted by the FBI. Intimidation was common. One former member has written that the FBI carried out over three thousand actions against the SDS ranging from beatings to planting drugs.[27] In some cases the FBI instructed the police conduct harassment. In Uptown, a minister affiliated with southern white youth was arrested on a suspicious drug charge. George Morey, a Presbyterian minister and founder of the Friendship House for southern white street teens, was arrested after a police raid on his apartment and found marijuana.[28] The charges were so preposterous that the Raleigh Campbell of the Chicago Southern Center publically came to Morey's defense. Campbell concluded that Morey had allied himself too closely with JOIN. Despite incidents such as these, JOIN continued to carve out a unique niche by giving voice to the poorest in Uptown. The rhetoric against police brutality became a self-fulfilling prophecy. As southern white migrants questioned and protested police tactics in their neighborhood, the answer came from the end of a billy club.

Ideas about class and inequality made sense to migrants, many of whom had lived in coal towns or seen the effects of mechanization. Organizers of JOIN succeeded in cultivating indigenous leaders among southern white migrants. They began with problems that southern whites experienced in Uptown, and interpreted them as universal problems of the poor. While inclined to read Fanon's, *The Wretched of the Earth*, migrants understood the workings of a company town. When people were organized around a rent strike, members of JOIN may have taken time to convey ideas about exploitation, for example. In doing so, JOIN left a blueprint of opposition for migrants to follow. By 1969, many student activists were drawn into larger national causes and devoted less attention to Uptown. However, the ideology of opposition was continued by the indigenous leadership there. Southern white migrants like Chuck Geary and Virginia Bowers were very active in JOIN and later in Uptown. Well into her sixties, Virginia Bowers has continued to be active in community organizing in Uptown. Sarah Dotson was one of the cofounders of the Chicago Area Black Lung Association, which fought for black lung claims of displaced miners and their widows. As many displaced miners in Uptown, Sarah's husband died from the effects of black lung disease before receiving any benefits.

In time other organizations emerged fight for the poor in Uptown. Some were a direct outgrowth of JOIN. One of the first was the Uptown Area Peoples Planning Coalition (UAPPC) in 1969. This multiracial coalition of the poor in Uptown protected their neighborhood against incursion by outside developers and the city. Led by Kentuckian, Charles "Chuck" Geary, the UAPPC voiced opposition to urban renewal and other social causes through a community newsletter, the *Uptown Light*, throughout the seventies.[29] Instead of cultural themes, their rhetoric centered around forming a class-based movement in Uptown. They couched their pleas for unity in class terms using a threat to the freedom of the poor. They petitioned Mayor Daley for direct representation on the Chicago Committee on Urban Opportunity (CCUO).[30] Geary, also directed the federally funded Tri-Faith Employment Center on Wilson Avenue. Tri-Faith concentrated on finding permanent jobs for the unemployed. He was a pragmatist who realized the futility of dreaming of going back to the South. He believed that people were "kidding themselves" when they spoke of returning to the South. Geary was a poster child for the southern white migrants. He had hitchhiked to Chicago after the Korean War after having shuttled tens of families to Uptown from Kentucky in his car. He was also an ordained minister. In an interview with the Chicagoan Magazine in 1968 he described his first trip to Chicago. "It looked good so I hitchhiked up. Slept on Montrose beach the first night to save my last two bucks, and met this guy drinkin" wine told me about a daily pay joint on Madison Street. After a week of daily work and busriddin' I had me twenty dollars. I went home sold near everything we had, loaded up our '37 Ford and a came back north." By the time of the interview, Geary lived in Uptown with his wife and eight children.[31]

The UAPPC concentrated efforts on resisting urban renewal. By 1970, 273 apartments had been demolished through urban renewal, and there were plans to destroy at least 1000 more, with no plans for replacement housing. To make matters worse, there was an influx of derelicts from the West Madison Street Skid Row urban renewal effort. To some there were daily changes in the neighborhood as these degenerates and mentally ill men panhandled and drank on corners. This exacerbated the poverty and homelessness in Uptown. Moreover, it conflated the image of the southern white migrant with that of the skid row drunk. For the casual observer, the media-driven stereotypes of southern whites were confirmed when they saw throngs of disheveled men with wine bottles sitting in doorways. By this time business leaders such as James Cain, vice-president of the Uptown Federal Savings and Loan, realized that the problem was not migrants but vagrants who had streamed into the area. "The southern whites are not the problem. It's these bums and day labor centers going up like popcorn stands."[32] For those concerned with the social and economic plight of Uptown this was not good news. For business leaders like Cain this only meant further erosion of the tax base and viability of local financial institutions.

Chuck Geary worked to halt displacement of the poor. In 1968, Project I of the Uptown Conservation Plan was unveiled by the UCC. Of particular concern to activists such as Geary was the plan to relocate a city community college right in the heart of the southern white neighborhood. The plan called for the razing of 4,000 units of low income housing, and with them many of his kinsmen and their families.[33] These families also represented a significant power base for Geary. If they went so would his ability to get the attention of developers and the city administration. The UCC supported the construction of the plan. To them it was a convenient way to rid Uptown of the rabble, and the southern white families inhabiting the area. Opposing this plan was Geary's Uptown Area People's Planning Coalition (UAPPC) an umbrella group that included numerous organizations in Uptown. Working with architect Rodney Wright, they developed an alternative plan for Hank Williams Village, a planned community with subsidized apartments, a pharmacy, and employment agency.[34] Geary was supported by other newer groups in Uptown composed of former JOIN members and other activists. The Voice of the People (VOP) and the Intercommunal Survival Committee argued that the plan would disrupt thousands of southern white families.[35] The UCC and local businesses agreed that the housing families would be displaced, but claimed that the housing was too shoddy to save. They also opposed the idea for Hank Williams Village. Geary's alternative plan was never realized. Buildings were condemned, land was cleared and Harry S. Truman College was built in 1976. This was a major blow to the southern whites in Uptown. In effect, it extracted the nucleus of the southern white community. To aggravate matters, the area suffered throughout the period as slum clearance, fires, and abandonment claimed buildings. Between 1970 and 1976, 1,200 units of low income housing were destroyed on the site to make way for the college. Arson evictions were common. When activists opposed mass evictions by organizing tenants to resist, their building would suddenly burn down. One tactic of landlords was to move unstable tenants into the building to terrorize residents. Those who remained were driven out by arson. Slumlords were cashing in on the redevelopment frenzy brought on by the relocation of the community college in Uptown. One building was torched 15 times in four months. Between 1975 and 1979 alone, fifteen buildings operated by the same individual were destroyed by fire.[36] Those displaced either moved out of Uptown to affordable areas, or went back to the South. In effect, much of the community was burned or driven out of the area. Part of the problem that Geary faced rested in the lack of community in Uptown. By this time there were Latinos, Native Americans, African Americans, southern whites and middle-class residents all living in close proximity. However, there was not one umbrella organization representing all the residents to give the community direction.

Nevertheless, a significant victory was reached with the Avery suit beginning in 1975. The plan to develop a forty-story tower apartment building (Pensacola Place) at the corner of Montrose and Sheridan was met with a class action lawsuit. Similar tactics were used to clear the block of buildings on the site. By that time, another organization, the Heart of Uptown Coalition (HOUC) had emerged as the most aggressive advocate of the poor led by Slim Coleman, former SDS member. Coleman charged Mayor Daley and developers with conspiring to "destroy" a poor community.[37] Given the evidence above, such an accusation held sway with many in the neighborhood. The litigation dragged on until 1988 when it was resolved to the partial satisfaction to the plaintiffs. The agreement included the allocation of 50 Section 8 subsidized housing in the proposed high rise apartment building, preference to former site residents, $45,000 in compensation to site residents, and the construction of a Jewel grocery store on the site.[38] Subsequently, the Department of Housing and Urban Development (HUD) was named in the suit with the Chicago Housing Authority. The death of Mayor Harold Washington in 1987, an ally of HUOC resulted in a less than adequate resolution to the suit.[39] Mayor Washington had been elected with significant support from the poor in Uptown. Slim Coleman and other members of the Heart of Uptown Coalition claimed credit for mobilizing a large coalition of poor voters to elect Washington. Washington acknowledged the support he had from Colemen and the HUOC, which gave Coleman and others access to City Hall until the Mayor's sudden death while in office in 1987.

In all, lives were lost, and property was destroyed through arson and radical gentrification. Resistance to this was born in southern white neighborhoods among a group who had struggled to survive against larger forces of decline and forced change in their community. By the middle 1960s, officials in Chicago faced a growing migrant population replenished regularly by newcomers from the South. In the shadow of the conspicuous wealth near the lake, migrants lived in shoddy conditions eking out an existence. What was particularly salient about Uptown was the proximity to wealth. By simply walking several blocks east, a newcomer could be in front of a castle-like home towering over a wrought iron fence that kept visitors out.

Officials in Chicago realized that inadequate housing, poor schools, high mobility, and unemployment that characterized the southern white neighborhood had to be alleviated. However, because of initial hostile treatment, migrants were suspicious of official organizations and tended to dislike outsiders. This was not something imbedded in culture per se, but a reaction to the hostility they received in Chicago. One important effect of JOIN was that they provided a social conduit and a framework for protest. This helped migrants take to the streets in defense of their neighborhood. They reshaped the issues and shifted the blame away from southern white migrants. Rather than moral or cultural failings, migrants realized that some of their appalling conditions had origins in social forces set in motion before their arrival. In the process some migrants realized that they shared similarities with all poor people. Whether they had been economically displaced or had come willingly, they were inspired to take action.

The baneful existence that many migrants endured contributed substantially to the saliency of JOIN. Southerners would not have participated in marches against police brutality had the police not subjected them to unofficial martial law and routine harassment. Similarly, overcrowding may have been tolerated if not for the substandard conditions of many apartments. Aging structures, years of neglect, and poor conversions made many apartments uninhabitable. JOIN offered southern families hope for the future. They believed that their lives would improve by participating in protest activities. By doing so, they strengthened their attachment to Uptown. Each battle, whether won or lost, had an effect of grounding the participants in the sense of giving them a piece of their neighborhood. It was an active process rather than simply applying for public aid. Both parties benefitted by engaging in social protest. Southern whites saw direct gains made by their efforts. The students of JOIN experienced the sense of accomplishment as proof that the revolution was possible on a small scale. It was an exchange relationship. If an apartment could be emptied of rats by a rent strike, southerners would participate. If this in turn furthered the political goals of JOIN so much the better. Few mentioned the degree to which a population could be energized by events involving social protest. When I interviewed Raleigh Campbell, he was critical of the student activists because of their lack of authenticity. He felt that they were patronizing southerners by acting or dressing like them. He seemed to think that members of JOIN were faking an affinity with southerners in order to further their goals. Campbell was the real deal. He was from Kentucky. He had an intuitive understanding of southern migrants. He could go into an apartment in Uptown with the ease of visiting one of his aunts back home. He joked about the student activists dressing in bib overalls of stereotypical southern clothing. He could see through this guise of familiarity. I think that southern migrants saw through this as well. Many were from isolated communities in Kentucky and West Virginia, and astute at recognizing strangers. Perhaps the students did not realize this. It was unimportant to the migrants as long as they saw tangible results to their protest, even if it meant simply rattling the cage of a landlord or the police to make their presence known.

An indirect result of the social resistance of the 1960s is a legacy of protest in Uptown. As efforts at gentrification continued throughout the years, so have remnants of this resistance movement. Since the 1960s, land use has been vigorously contested by many groups with competing views of Uptown's future. Few if any proposals for redevelopment, zoning variances or new business have gone uncontested. It is an oversimplification to characterize these skirmishes as the rich against the poor. Nevertheless, development has often involved the poor being displaced to make way for more affluent residents. Since the 1970s, grass roots organizations like the Intercommunal Survival Committee (ISC), the Voice of the People (VOP), the Heart of Uptown Coalition (HOUC), the Chicago Area Black Lung Association (CABLA), and the Uptown People's Law Center, have been active in tenant's rights, black lung claims and legal representation of the poor.

Since the 1970s southern whites have been eclipsed by other new arrivals in Uptown. Today, some children of southern white migrants have continued to fight for the poor and the powerless in Uptown be they second generation southern whites or newly arrived immigrants from Central America. As in other cities urban renewal was based on eradication of existing housing. Few failed to realize the effect this would have on existing communities. Although the voices in some cities had little representation or clout, the voice of the people in Uptown was vigorously expressed by groups which emerged in the 1960s with strains remaining today. Though large projects such as the construction of Truman College removed thousands of residents, the strand of resistance in Uptown continues.

Notes

1. Migrant, Margaret Jamison, quoted in Todd Gitlin and Nanci Hollander, *Uptown: Poor Whites in Chicago* (New York: Harper and Row, 1970), 304.
2. "Deny Alliance with JOIN" *Edgewater-Uptown News,* 17 November 1965, 1(N).
3. "The Port Huron Statement," in *Takin' it to the Streets, ed.* Alexander Bloom and Eini Breines (New York: Oxford University Press, 1995), 61–74.

4. Ralph McGill, "Poverty's White Ghetto Face," *Charleston Gazette-Mail,* 10 October 1966, 9(N), "Southern White Migrants in Slums Fail to Benefit From Anti-Poverty Drive."*The Wall Street Journal,* 30 September 1965.

5. John Kasarda, "Caught in the Web of Change." *Society,* (November and December, 1983),44–54.

6. Personal interview by the author with Edward Kennedy, Chicago Department of Human Services, 15 March 1994.

7. Chuck Geary quoted is from an untitled portion of an article. *Chicago Land Magazine* (July 1968): 35–39.

8. William Julius Wilson, *The Declining Significance of Race: Blacks and Changing American Institutions* (Chicago: University of Chicago Press, 1978), 67.

9. "The Chicago Plan," (Chicago Commission on Urban Opportunity, June 1966):x

10. Michael Harrington, *The Other America: Poverty in the United States* (New York: Penguin, 1972).

11. Chicago Commission on Urban Opportunity. "The Chicago Plan: Supplementary Report on Unemployed Males," Cook County Department of Public Aid, Illinois State Employment Service, June 1966.

12. John Charles Boger, "Race and the American City: The Kerner Commission in Retrospect - An Introduction," *North Carolina Law Review* 71, no. 3 (1993):1289–1349.

13. "Race and the American City"

14. "War on Slums Begins," *Edgewater Uptown News.* 22 December 1965, 1(N).

15. "Harried Landlord Bows," *Edgewater-Uptown News,* 24 May 1966, 1(N).

16. "Harried Landlord Bows."

17. "Rats vs. Family: Dad Needs Rifle," *Edgewater-Uptown News,* 16 March 1965, 1(N).

18. "JOIN Claims Victory After Day-long Picket." *Edgewater-Uptown News,* 8 February 1966, 1(N).

19. "New Office Unites Home Inspectors," *Edgewater-Uptown News,* 30 March 1965.

20. Personal interview by the author with Virginia Bowers, 15 March 1994

21. "Uptown Council Leader to Talk with Dissidents over Membership," *Chicago Tribune,* 3 August 1967.

22. "They Marched, They talked, They," *Edgewater Uptown News,* 16 August 1966, 2(N). Subsequent investigations revealed a theft ring among police at that particular station. The basement was full of stolen goods.

23. Interviewee wished to remain anonymous.

24. Gitlin and Hollander *Uptown: Poor Whites in Chicago,* 387.

25. See for example, "North Side Tavern Hit in Raids" *Edgewater-Uptown News,* 7 June 1966,2 (N). "Defends JOIN after Vice Party Charges," *Edgewater-Uptown News,* 25 June 1965, "Fire Guts JOIN Office," *Edgewater-Uptown News,* 15 February 1966, Gitlin and Nanci Hollander, *Uptown: Poor Whites in Chicago,* 375–398.

26. In May of 1996 a southern woman died in her apartment. When police arrived, they reportedly took her corpulent, naked body out of the apartment in full view of neighbors and her children. They also ate food from her apartment and played video games. Personal observation by the author.

27. Michael Rossman, "Notes from an SDS Reunion," <http://sds.revolt.org/Rossman.htm> (22 December 2006).

28. Ruth Anderson, "Deny Alliance with JOIN "*Edgewater-Uptown News,* 17 November 1965, 1(N).

29. Although widely discussed by informants, only one copy of the *Uptown Light* could be located at the Chicago Historical Society.

30. Petition from the UAPPC to Mayor Daley, dated August 11, 1969, Department of Public Aid files, Cook County.

31. Untitled excerpt from *Chicagoan Magazine* 5, no. 9 (July 1968): 37.

32. "Uptown's Poor - Are They Victims of Urban Renewal?" *Chicago Sun-Times,* 5 October 5, 1970, 5(N).

33. Karen Zaccor, "Uptown's 15 year Battle in the Gentrification War," *Keep Strong* 8, No.3 (September/October 1987):35.

34. "Hank Williams Lives in Uptown." *Lerner Booster,* 12 July 1968, 4 (N).

35. Thomas M. Gray, "Planned Razing to Displace Unknown Number in Uptown." *Chicago Sun Times,* 23 June 1970.

36. "Uptown's 15 year Battle in the Gentrification War," 6.

37. "Uptown Group Charges High Rise Plot," *Chicago Tribune,* 9 October 1975.

38. "Uptown Developer Back in Court." *Chicago Tribune*, 5 August 1982.

39. "Judge Ok's Renter's Suit Settlement," *Chicago Tribune,* 8 December 1987.

Chapter 7

The Migrant Generation:
From Unity to Invisibility

It is so stressful to live in this neighborhood now. You got drug dealers, you got gangs, you got crooked police. Most of the people from the South I knew are either gone or dead.[1]

Only strands of the southern migration still remain in Uptown. They are woven into the melange of the diverse social fabric that composes the neighborhood today. Each day that I rode my bicycle through Uptown on my way to interview someone from the South. I passed a house on Magnolia where a women sat on her porch smoking. Once I saw an older man on the porch in a white tee-shirt with faded tattoos. Although I have never met them, I know that they are among the small group of southerners who remain in Uptown. Clara Belcher still lives with her daughter in a building occupied by a handful of other southern families. On most days you can find Clara walking down Broadway near Montrose, once the core of the Southern neighborhood. She used to walk to the Jewell supermarket with her friend Violet before she passed away. Clara tells me that she recognizes few faces amidst the throngs of have-nots standing in front of the Salvation Army distribution center. Further down at the corner of Broadway and Montrose people score dope from a rolling dealer in a white Buick Rivera. After completing this work Sarah Dotson died in the company of her family on Sunnyside Avenue. She never made it back to West Virginia. Just west of Uptown on Ainslie Street, Former JOIN member Virginia Bowers has a small apartment. She continues to volunteer in an elementary school in Uptown. The architects who worked on Hank Williams Village, Rodeny and Sidney Wright now live in Kentucky. The charismatic visionary, behind the Village, Chuck Geary faded into obscurity. He died in Texas without realizing his dream of a southern town in the middle of Chicago.

Over the years, efforts at resisting the displacement of affordable housing had limited success. Activists were unable to prevent the larger forces of change in the community. Since the 1970s southerners were displaced to other neighborhoods with the construction of Truman College and Pensacola Place. Recently there has been a slow reconquest of Uptown by affluent singles and some daring couples with children. Most of these urban pioneers have purchased condominiums that were converted from some older three flat apartments on Maldon and Beacon streets. This sort of gentrification makes many streets of Uptown unaffordable to the poor of all colors. Virginia Bowers was forced to move into an adjacent neighborhood because of the lack of affordable housing in Uptown. Some of the condominiums resemble mini-gated communities that Mike Davis wrote about in *City of Quartz*. However the residences of these new urbanites could be in any city in America. Steel fences extend to the sidewalk with intercoms into which those desiring admittance must request permission. Cameras peer down from the corners of some buildings on unsuspecting pedestrians. As for the southern migrants, there has been a selective migration out of Uptown. The more successful migrants moved to the suburbs or went to the South. Others are gone to their rest in Graceland Cemetery, which is visible from the Belcher apartment.[2]

Although census data indicates nearly 20 percent of Uptown's population is from the South, it is nearly impossible to find a southern migrant amid the throngs of Vietnamese, Nigerians, and Mexicans roaming the streets of Uptown. As Helen Elam's comment above points out, danger reins in some areas of Uptown. It is probable that some of those from the South are simply too poor to leave. Others, remain because their children and friends. Perhaps those that remain in Chicago simply want to believe that the option to return home exists. Helen tried to back to Tennessee several times but was unable to make a living. When asked whether he would ever return to the South, Donald Powell was forced to acknowledge that heartache and misery prevented him from going back. The rehabilitation of apartments to condominiums has resulted in a shortage or affordable rental apartments. Some of those that remain like Clara Belcher are only waiting for their buildings to be sold and are unsure about the future.[3] While some speak of a suburban exodus of southerners from Uptown, there is little proof other than census figures that show a decline in the white population in Uptown. Families lucky enough to receive black lung benefits or settlements used them to move out of Uptown. For all the numerous reasons, opportunities, and motivation that brought southerners to Chicago, there are an equal number that resulted in them leaving. More than a mass exodus, southerners have trickled out of the neighborhood.

The traditional explanation states that the majority came as a result of technological changes in traditional methods of work. Thousands of people were displaced from work due to the mechanization of mining or farming. Seen this way we are left with the impression that most of our lives are determined by forces much beyond our control. Though social forces are instrumental in shaping our lives, people respond to them in different ways. Chicago for many migrants was an inadvertent destination. Some came on a whim to a place they'd heard about from friends and kin who had gone and returned. A lot of adventuresome southerners simply wanted to see hillbilly heaven. They wanted to experience what the others talked about. They longed for a taste of Wilson Avenue. Like Violet McKnight who wanted to experience urban life, these migrants wanted to escape in some ways. Fatal mining and farming accidents had snatched loved ones from them leading them to seek better lives for their families. Others were simply unwilling or unable to take the place of their fathers and brothers in the mines. While some departed reluctantly, all had a dream of something better in Chicago. In some sense those southerners in Uptown were the lucky ones. They were able to leave.

Because so many left involuntarily, the migrant generation carried a strong attachment to home. Home was omnipresent. Migrants were reminded of their birthplace when they spoke to outsiders and other southerners. They lived in a state of limbo as long as they remained in the North. Although the migrants had diverse origins, home as a metaphor emerged in similar form in Chicago. The South became an enigmatic place to which they would someday return if only just to be buried. Persisting toil and tribulation in Chicago would be rewarded by a final trip to the South. Some like Sarah Dotson never made it. My guess is that those that remain in Uptown will never make that final journey. The tendency to romanticize home was less intense among women. While men enjoyed a more dominant status at home, women were often subjugated to traditional roles in the home and often controlled with force. Women differed from men in their ambiguity about the North. Whereas men spoke often about their desire to return, women expressed this desire in more specific terms preferring to cite reunification with kinfolk and friends. Men, however, preferred to concentrate on the activities and freedom they enjoyed in the past. For men looking at the South meant looking at the past. Many migrants sought to recreate the South in the North. For others, the opportunity for independence and anonymity represented a powerful counter balance to the nostalgia of home. Women could work, socialize more freely, and gain distance from traditional bonds imposed at home. Men had more opportunity for work and were free from the more constraining aspects of small town.

Migration forced choices on southerners. All had expectations of Chicago. All were affected by the urban experience. Remaining in Chicago meant committing to change. It meant accepting separation from their places of origin. It meant comparing these two places perpetually throughout their lives. For years some would live in two places at once. They were disillusioned with the urban experience, yet they had no viable place to return. Migration meant passing a legacy onto their children of a place frozen in time, a place of their generation. By doing so the migrant generation passed an identity onto the children and instilled in them a desire to return. Home was always beckoning. It was present in popular culture, it was conjured up in conversations, it was imposed on them by Chicagoans, it was easily reached. This idea of home for southern whites differed from that of African Americans who came to Chicago. In James Grossman's words, southern blacks thought of Chicago as a "land of hope."[4] Southern whites were more ambiguous about their destination. They seemed to want to return to the South of yesterday, while southern blacks want to return to the South of today. For whites, Chicago presented a set of constraints. There were no failed conditions of emancipation in their social landscape. There was no Jim Crow. There was social preeminence in the South for white southerners. Unlike some of the bonds and solidarity that race afforded African Americans, however oppressive, white southerners were not prepared for the debilitating stereotypes and treatment they endured in Chicago. This caused a loss of status relative to that enjoyed in the South. Compared to southern blacks the process of community formation and unity for whites began in the North. The unity was reinforced by common experiences in Uptown.

Part of this idea of being southern in terms of one's identity in Chicago meant reevaluating ideas about race. Most had never seen black and whites interact on anything resembling equal terms in a social setting, nor had previous social contact with other races. Some embraced the new racial ambiance while others clung to their views and resisted the tendency toward change. In general women responded more positively to the new racial order than men. Men experienced a loss of racial and gender status they enjoyed in the South. To be a southern white man in Chicago then meant accommodating albeit reluctantly to this loss of status. Of course law and custom left few any choice.

As southern white neighborhoods grew, so did the negative media accounts. Most relied on an atavistic mountaineer prototype first developed in the nineteenth century by northern magazine writers. Migrants were portrayed as filthy, incestuous fornicators driven only by the desire for liquor, sex, and cars. These stories left the impression that the only cause for southern migrant poverty was their own venal instincts. Their accounts fueled prejudice against those trying to gain a foothold in the urban economy. This resulted in exaggerated fears about southerners as criminals and malcontents. It conveniently separated migrants from the mainstream culture and made them an aberration explained only by genes and an isolated sub-culture rather than the failure of a system which valued labor as a commodity. Southerners responded to this by defending their neighborhood which reinforced their unity and southern identity.

The suburban flight of industry, and declining wages for entry-level positions forced an enduring cycle of dependence on many migrants. This was aggravated by an increased reliance on a growing daily-pay sector of temporary employment in low-wage, light industrial work throughout the sixties. Complicating this were powerful groups of citizens and developers in Uptown bent on urban renewal. The large spacious apartments were no longer profitable to operate, and were in serious decay. Renewal efforts were hampered by large numbers of southern newcomers and a shortage of affordable replacement housing. The search for profit from aging buildings led to unprecedented conversions to more concentrated living arrangements. Southerners occupied these flats in large numbers. Uptown was evolving into a low income community with local businesses trying to keep pace. The historic role of Uptown as an entertainment district left many taverns and cheap hotels. This aggravated the problems of the growing population of southern whites. Rather than a port of entry in which migrants were processed and accommodated, Uptown was becoming a holding tank for the poor and aggrieved. Coupled with this was an increasing homeless population displaced from other neighborhoods. Wealthier citizens and business leaders were allied in a struggle to reverse this decline, and they concentrated on efforts to rid Uptown of the poor residents, many of whom were southern migrants.

In this climate of fear it was easy to portray southerners as the cause of urban decay. They were an unorganized group of newcomers. Being new to Chicago left southern migrants vulnerable negative depictions. The Chicago Southern Center (CSC) and Jobs or Income Now (JOIN) helped organize the migrants into a force for change. The CSC instilled a sense of pride in southern migrants. Raleigh Campbell and William Meyers campaigned for positive treatment of southerners in the media, and showed that many migrants were capable workers and residents, given the chance. The center called attention to the difficulties that migrants faced when arriving in Chicago. The programs were aimed at providing a leg up for struggling families beginning their life in Uptown. In addition cultural activities affirmed positive aspects of southern identity. Music, quilting, and visits by southern authors reminded migrants of the positive contributions made by southerners to American culture. In this way divisions of county and region no longer mattered. A common southern heritage took shape much like other ethnic groups adopted an identity based on nationality. I am not suggesting that strong antagonisms existed along county lines among southerners. I am arguing that recognizable differences were effaced and replaced by a unity that consisted of being from the South. Although less political than JOIN, the CSC made important inroads toward migrant representation and advocacy. It also created a conduit which other social service agencies used to reach migrants. It is doubtful that JOIN would have experienced the degree of success that it did in such a short period of time without the early efforts of the CSC.

The CSC reached migrants by active community participation by the CSC staff like Raleigh Campbell. Southerners were reluctant to seek any sort of aid and were weary of outsiders. Campbell knew from the onset that they would have to walk the streets to reach the southerners. He was also confident that being from Kentucky would strengthen his ability to communicate to migrants. By soliciting their needs they developed programs which attracted significant numbers of southern migrants. Eventually southern migrants learned to take advantage of opportunities available in Uptown. Together with lobbying efforts by the Chicago Southern Center, and the heavy social clout of W. Clement Stone, journalists began to write favorable stories about migrans. Instead of portraying the southern migrant as a lazy drunkard, the writers suggested that the migrant was striving for a better life though hard work and sobriety. The Boys Club in Uptown brought needed health care and recreation to migrant children through innovative services involving community outreach. Even by contemporary standards, there are few if any programs that match the community health programs offered though the Robert R. McCormick Boys Club in Uptown. By 1970 thousands of children had received free dental care, vision tests and physical examinations.

Children fared somewhat better than their parents, many of whom continued to struggle with substandard housing, poverty wages, and police brutality. Buildings had been neglected by landlords. Many apartments in Uptown were uninhabitable by city standards. Slack code enforcement added to the intractable problem of shoddy low-cost housing. The arrival of JOIN in 1964 marked the beginning of an era of community activism that persisted though the 1990s. Although highly criticized by city officials JOIN raised public awareness about migrants' conditions by using newly emerging tactics of social protest. Rent strikes, marches, and direct confrontation forced city inspectors to take notice of the housing problem. This pressured landlords to begin to repair some buildings. JOIN helped southern migrants to form councils to settle tenant-landlord disagreements. In this way many disputes were through informal arbitration rather than official means. This led to compromises which suited the landlord and the tenants. Southerners supported efforts by JOIN. Some like Virginia Bowers took a stand against landlords even if it meant losing her position as a building manager. When Uptown was slated for large-scale urban renewal, a structure was in place for organized resistance. Although much of the rhetoric was couched in terms of the oppression of those with the least power to resist, officials could seldom ignore the coalition of southern migrants. JOIN showed migrants that if they stuck together they could be a formidable force if they mobilized quickly for a protest. The student activists taught southern migrants to hold police accountable for their heavy-handed tactics and brutality. Using tactics from the Black Panthers, officers were watched by the groups of southerners who asked for badge numbers and took pictures. Although much of this resistance was met with retaliation by police, the southerners made a point. As in Watts, Oakland, and other urban areas people in the community demonstrated that they were unwilling to tolerate hostile and unequal treatment by the police. It was through struggle that a sense of community and solidarity developed among migrants throughout the sixties.

One direct outgrowth of grassroots activism was the emergence of southern leaders such as, Chuck Geary. The formation of the Uptown Area Peoples Planning Coalition (UAPPC) in 1969 was a sign that southern migrants were taking ownership of their community. This coalition of the poor in Uptown was formed in response to urban renewal efforts of the Uptown Chicago Commission (UCC) Established in 1957, the UCC had close ties with Mayor Richard Daley and the financial support of important Uptown businesses. Led by Chuck Geary, the UAPPC resisted urban renewal and developments that would displace poor residents. Geary insisted that the poor be represented on the local renewal board, the Uptown Community Conservation Council (CCC).[5]

Geary worked to halt the demolition of housing occupied by the poorer residents in Uptown. In 1968, a project was unveiled by the Community Conservation Council to build a Harry S. Truman community college in Uptown. The original plan called for the razing of 4,000 units of low income housing in Uptown. Geary and the UAPPC opposed this plan to level more buildings. Working with architect Rodney Wright, UAPPC developed an alternative plan for Hank Williams Village, a project for the poor patterned after a southern town Geary envisioned the complex having a job center, pharmacy and grocery shopping.[6] Geary's alternative plan was never realized. By 1970, 273 apartments had been demolished, with plans to destroy at least a 1,000 more units. Added to this was the assurance that the poor would be permanently displaced from Uptown. There were no plans for replacement housing.[7] This would insure that the southern population in Uptown would diminish, and along with it some of Geary's power base.

The displacement of southerners triggered by the construction of Harry S. Truman college in the 1970s marked the beginning of the end of their presence in Uptown. Whole blocks of large buildings in which thousands of southern whites lived were razed to make way for the college. The residents' protests fell on deaf ears. Similarly, the construction of Pensacola Place in the 1980s displaced another large group of southern whites. "Where Truman College is now, that was all leveled. That area and where Pensacola Place is at Montrose and Broadway used to be solid southern white."[8] These families scattered to other parts of the city, more distant suburbs or back home.

There is little agreement among community representatives, or even the remaining southerners, as to exactly where they went. Certainly no official sources charted their trajectory or whereabouts. In general, people can only tell you where their friends or relatives relocated. The rest is left to speculation. The observer cited above believed that most were squeezed west toward the area of Albany Park by gentrification advancing north from Lakeview, and south from the area around Loyola University. In his view the area near Kedzie and Lawrence west of Uptown is what Wilson and Broadway used to be thirty years ago. Former SDS member and a community activist, Slim Colemen, claims that southern whites went to the suburbs.[9] Still others believe that some returned to the South after receiving settlements claims for black lung benefits.[10] Some may argue more vociferously than others, but when it is all done the evidence reveals a pronounced decline of southern whites in Uptown. For example in 1960 over 80 percent of the population in census tract 320 were born in the South. By 2000 this had declined to less than 4 percent. Other areas of Uptown reflect similar declines.[11]

While southerners arrived in large waves throughout the fifties and sixties, they have departed in a similar fashion since then. Sharp declines are revealed with the publication of each decennial census. With the loss of each building to arson or gentrification southerners have left Uptown. Some had little choice, given the paucity of replacement housing. Little by little the events chipped away at the numbers of southerners in Uptown. Whereas the evolution of the community by the early period made Uptown a natural port of entry for southern whites, the location and condition of housing also made it attractive for gentrification today. Uptown's proximity to Lake Michigan and Lincoln Park make Uptown extremely coveted domain by redevelopers. Just as the larger restructuring of agriculture and mining set southerners in motion earlier, the forces of gentrification had the same effect beginning in the 1970s. Southerners were forced to repeat this process of migration once again. For those pushed out of the community, however, there were few kinsmen to pave the way, no fledgling community in which to flock, and no promise of jobs. Instead they must rely on social security, pensions, and an economy increasingly tilted toward the better educated and the young.

As mentioned, most southern migrants have left Uptown. The few buildings with southern migrants are located mostly by word of mouth. Moreover, they are reluctant to discuss the past. The first time that I asked Billy Belcher to discuss his story of migration from the South he shut the door before I had finished talking. It seems that those who remain are the unlucky ones. Southerners were once a force in Uptown. Though they still lay claim to their neighborhood, few newcomers to Uptown respect this or understand the history behind this. As with much of the original architecture southerners are showing signs of age or have been replaced by newer arrivals. They look forward to leaving but have no means or are hindered by those who remain. Their spouses are buried nearby, their grand children are growing up in Chicago, or they have no kin in the South. Women are more represented among the southerners that remain in Uptown. Their men have died from the effects of years in the mines, the steel mills of Chicago, hard drinking, and a rough life in general. While living in the area, I have been hit up on the street for money in the morning by a southerner so drunk that he had trouble standing. However, I have also spent countless hours in the living room of another Billy Belcher who quit the hard life to survive. The difference between these two is not their southern roots, but the effect migration has had on the individual. While both were affected by the social forces that loosened the population their lives have had very different trajectories. It was only by examining their lives in the past, and having the patience to be attentive to the nuances of their lives that I understand both men.

Architecturally in Uptown few remnants of the past remain. The Uptown theater, a symbol of postmodernism, lies vacant, deteriorated and for rent since 1982.[12] The white ornate facade is graffiti-ridden and looks oddly old, spent and skeletal across the street from the Mr. Goodyear shop with signs hawking brake jobs for foreign cars. Bruce Springsteen was the last person to perform there. Recently there are efforts to restore the structure to its original state. Three doors down the infamous Green Mill lounge is host to a new group of jazz-crazy youth sporting nose rings and tatoos. It is still one of the best places in Chicago to catch jazz after hours. Because relatively little has changed inside the Green Mill, it has been the site of several movies; including "The Thief" with James Caan and more recently "High Fidelity" with John Cusak. The Riviera theater, a popular night spot throughout the first half of the century, continues to operate hosting punk, funk and rap palace. The interior still features a wildly-ornate interior made all the more startling by the purple, green and gold paint-job done in the 1970s. The incumbent alderwoman, Helen Shiller, used it as a rallying point for special activities, marches, and the victory celebration for her campaign workers in a recent election. The Aragon Ballroom is one of Chicagos last surviving dance halls that remained open in the 1990s. Instead of Benny Goodman the Aragon features two to three shows per week ranging from Mexican Norteño bands to rock. It was the last venue played by the band Nirvana.

The demographic changes in Uptown are equally astonishing and make Uptown unrecognizable to many southern migrants who return to the old neighborhood. Since 1950, the racial composition of Uptown has changed. When most of the southern migrants arrived, the area was 97 percent white. Over time, however, African Americans, Latinos, and Southeast Asians have moved into the area. Whites made up less than 50 percent of the population as of 2000. While Uptown is recognized as one of the most diverse communities in Chicago, the minority population has declined recently. According to a recently land use study, nearly all of the census tracts experienced disproportionate losses in the African American population compared to the rest of the city of Chicago. Losses of population have also been seen in each major ethnic group except non-Hispanic whites. While the Asian and Hispanic populations of Chicago have grown dramatically, their population in Uptown declined. However, Uptown still has a higher proportion of whites and Asians than the city at large.[13] Social interaction in Uptown often reflected these trends. In the shadow of the Uptown theater's fire escape on Magnolia Street, I used to observe a remaining southern white family siting on their front porch watching their multi-colored neighbors walk up the street. On the corner of Glenwood and Argyle streets Asian youth dressed in hip-hop clothing sat on stoops, smoking and sizing-up pedestrians.

Population changes are indicative of larger trends which have brought many foreign-born migrants to Uptown and similar neighborhoods in other American cities. As a result Uptown now contains pockets of urban villages. Argyle Street and its environs are dubbed "Little Saigon." A large public housing project looms nearby with African American children in front. A growing sector of condominiums has attracted a number of urban professionals. The rate of increase in condominiums exceeds that of the rest of Chicago. The accelerated rate of condominium growth predictable given the history of Uptown's housing. During the 1990s the new condominiums lured those seeking to benefit from an anticipated upswing in the area. During this time, those older inhabitants who have stayed developed the bunker mentality characteristic of their peers in other cities. Older elegant homes are surrounded by black wrought iron and security cameras—a growing distinction between the rich and poor in Uptown.

When interviewed some southerners judged the non-white presence as indicative of the community's decline. Just as the arrival of southern whites was a prophecy of doom to wealthier residents in the past, the arrival of people of color foreshadowed the unraveling of order and spells decline. In both cases those in Uptown never considered the larger forces involved in migration. In both cases the local residents viewed the present from the lens of the past. Once the domain of southern migrants Uptown is now in the hands other newcomers. It remains to be seen whether this new gap between the rich and poor will result in conflict or cooperation. It seems certain that as long as the poor are viewed as expendable members of society, conflict will ensure.

Notes

1. Personal interview by the author with Helen Elam 18 December 1994.

2. In the course of writing this Clara's husband, Billy Belcher passed away.

3. Personal interview by the author with Clara Belcher, 15July 2005.

4. James Grossman, *Land of Hope: Chicago, Black Southerners and the Great Migration* (Chicago: University of Chicago Press, 1989)

5. Uptown Area People's Planning Coalition. A letter to Mayor Dailey, 1969. In the author's possession.

6. "Hank Williams 'Lives' in Uptown." *Lerner Booster,* 12 July 1968, 1(N).

7. "Uptown's Poor - Are They Victims of Urban Renewal?" *Chicago Sun-Times,* 5 October 1970, 5(N).

8. Personal interview by the author with Edward Kennedy, Department of Human Services, 2 February 1994.

9. Personal interview by the author with Walter "Slim" Colemen, March 1992.

10. Personal interview by the author with Lori Odell, 8 April 1992.

11. Peter Hass, Phillip Nyden, Thomas Walsh, Nathan Benefield and Christopher Giangreco, "The Uptown Housing and Land Use Study" (Unpublished report, The Center for Urban Research and Learning, Loyola University of Chicago, 2002).

12. Herron argued that a central feature of postmodernism is the presence of "end markers" in which premonitions of the future, catastrophic or redemptive, have been replaced by senses of the end of this or that." Jerry Heron, *Afterculture: Detroit and the Humiliation of History,* (Detroit: Wayne State University Press, 1993), 117. Frederic Jameson, *Postmodernism, or, the Cultural Logic of Late Capitalism.* (Durham, North Carolina: University of North Carolina Press, 1990).

13. "The Uptown Housing and Land Use Study."

Selected Bibliography

Oral Histories and Interviews:

Unless otherwise indicated all the interviews were conducted in Chicago by the author on the date indicated. Those without a date indicate on-going contact or interviews too numerous to list.

Belcher, Belinda. First interview, October 12, 1992.
Belcher, Clara.
Belcher, Billy.
Bowers, Virginia. March 18, 1994.
Campbell, Raleigh. Roanoke, Virginia, August 4, 1995.
Campbell, Rae Vonne. Roanoke, Virginia, August, 4 1995.
Coleman, "Slim" Walter. October 8, 1992.
Dickholtz, M. October 10, 1994.
Donnelson, John. March 19, 1994.
Dotson, Kenney. June 20, 1994.
Dotson, Sarah. June 20, 1994 and September 8, 1994.
Elam, Helen. December 18, 1994.
Hamilton, Randy. September 8, 1994.
Hanks, Ruby. September 8, 1994.
Johnson, Robert. Sergeant, Chicago Police, February 14, 1994
Johanson, Donald. Chicago Police Department, February 14, 1994.
Jones, Loyal. Berea, Kentucky, October 11, 1995.
Kenedy Edward. Chicago, Department of Human Services, February 2, 1994.
Lambert, James. June 29, 1994.
Lickerman, Fred. April 5, 1994.
McKnight, Violet. June 22, 1994.
Milne, Pat. Milwuakee, February 17, 1994.
Moore, Tom. April 20, 1994.
Moore, Ray. June 23, 1994.
Odell, Laurie. April 4, 1992.
Powell, Donald "Donnie." June 28, 1994.
Sadri, Cyris. January 10, 1994.
Seigel, Paul. June 10, 1992.
Shiller, Helen, Alderman 46th Ward, Chicago. March 2, 1994.

Sorenson, Walter. Centervile, Ohio, February 10, 1995.
Wells, Albert. October 7, 1994.
White, Elias. April 6, 1995.
Woods, Mary. September 12, 1994.

Newspapers

Atlanta Journal
Charleston Daily Gazzette, 1963–65.
Chicago Daily News, 1965–1966
Chicago Sun-Times, 1950–present
Chicago Tribune, 1950–present
Cinncinnati Enquirer
Dayton Hearld, 1959–1960
Detroit Free Press, 1959–1960
Edgewater-Uptown News, (*Uptown News*), 1957–1977
Hazard Herald, 1963
Louisville Courier-Journal, 1955–1965
Learner Booster
New York Times, 1960–1966
Wall Street Journal, 1960–66

Archives and Special Collections

Southern Appalachian Archives, Hutchins Library, Berea College, Berea Kentucky: Council of the Southern Mountains and Perley F. Ayer Collections.
Chicago Historical Society.
Ravenswood Historical Society, Sulzer Regional Library, Chicago.
Municipal Reference Collection: Chicago Public Library.

Books, Articles and Dissertations.

Anderson, Elijah. *Streetwise: Race, Class and Change in an Urban Community.* Chicago: University of Chicago Press, 1990.
Andres, Alfred. *History of Cook County Illinois.* (privately published 1884).
Arnow, Harriette. *The Dollmaker* New York: Macmillian, 1954.
Banks, Nancy. "The World's Most Beautiful Ballrooms," *Chicago History* 2, No. 4 (1970):206.
Berry, Chad. *Southern Migrants, Northern Exiles*. Urbanna, University of Illinois Press, 2000.
Beynon, Erdmon D. The Southern White Laborer Migrates to Michigan." *American Sociological Review* 3, No. 3 (1938):333–343.
Brown, James S. "Migration within to and from the Appalachians, 1935-1959: A Preliminary Report on the Southern Appalachian Studies Migration Project.

(unpublished report presented at Berea College,1959).

————. "The Family Behind the Migrant." *Mountain Life and Work* (September, 1968):4–7.

Brown, James S. and Clyde McCoy. "Appalachian Migration to Midwestern Cities." in William Phillibur and Clyde McCoy, eds., *The Invisible Minority: Urban Appalachians*. Lexington: University of Kentucky Press, 1984.

Brown, James, S. Harry K. Swarzweller and Joseph J. Mangalam. "Kentucky Mountain Migration and the Stem Family: An American Variation on the Theme by Le Play," *Rural Sociology*, 28, No. 1 (1963):48–69.

Brown, Malcolm and John N. Webb. *Seven Stranded Coal Towns*. New York: De Capo Press, 1971.

Bruno, Hal. "Chicago's Hillbilly Ghetto." in Hanna Meisser, ed., *Poverty in an Affluent Society*. New York: Harper and Row, 1964.

Burgess, Ernest. "The Growth of the City" in Robert Park, Ernest Burgess and Roderick D. McKenzie, *The City*. Chicago: University of Chicago Press, 1967.

Burgess, Ernest and Charles Newcomb, *Census Data for Chicago, 1930*, Chicago: University of Chicago Press, 1933.

Chicago Recreation Commission and Northwestern University. *The Chicago Recreation Survey, 1937*. Chicago: Chicago Recreation Commission and Northwestern University, 1930, p.38.

Chicago Fact Book Consortium, ed. *Local Community Fact Book*, Department of Sociology, University of Illinois-Chicago, 1985.

Chicago Commission on Urban Opportunity. "The Chicago Plan: Supplementary Report on Unemployed Males." Cook County Department of Public Aid, Illinois State Employment Service, June 1966.

Chicago Plan Commission. "Population Facts for Planning Chicago." Chicago: The Chicago Plan Commission, 1942.

Cohen, Norman. "The Skillet Lickers: A Study of the Hillbilly String Band and Its Repertoire" *Journal of American Folklore* Vol. 78, No. 308 (1965): 229–244.

Coles, Robert. *The South Goes North.* Boston: Little Brown, 1971.

Cook County Department of Public Aid. "The Southern Appalachian Migrant on Public Aid in Cook County: A Follow Up Study." (Unpublished report, Cook County Department of Public Aid, 1963).

Davis, James Leslie. *The Elevated System and the Growth of Northern Chicago*, Evanston, Illinois: Northwestern University Department of Geography, 1970.

Dodd, Donald B. and Wynelle S. Dodd, *Historical Statistics of the South, 1790-1970*. Birmingham: University of Alabama, 1973.

Ford, Thomas, ed. *The Southern Appalachian Region: A Survey*. Lexington: University of Kentucky Press, 1962.

Flynt, J. Wayne. *Dixie's Forgotten People: The South's Poor Whites* Bloomington: Indiana University Press, 1979.

————. *Poor But Proud: Alabama's Poor Whites*. Tuscaloosa: University of Alabama Press, 1989.

Franklin, Wayne and Michael Stiener, eds. *Mapping American Culture*. Iowa City:

University of Iowa Press, 1992.

Gagne, Patricia L. "Appalachian Women: Violence and Social Control" *Journal of Contemporary Ethnography* 20, No. 4, (January 1992):387–415).

Gaventa, John G., Barbara Ellen Smith and Alex Willingham, eds., *Communities in Economic Crisis: Appalachia and the South*. Philadelphia: Temple University Press, 1990.

Giesen, Carol A.B. *Coal Miners' Wives: Portraits of Endurance*. Lexington: The University Press of Kentucky, 1995.

Giffin, Roscoe. "From Cinder Hollow to Cincinnati" *Mountain Life and Work* Vol. 32 (1956):11-20.

Gitlin, Todd and Nanci Hollander. *Uptown: Poor Whites in Chicago*. New York: Harper and Row, 1970.

Green, Archie. 1965. "Hillbilly Music: Source and Symbol." *Journal of American Folklore* Vol. 78 No. 308 (1965):204–228.

Gregory, James N. *American Exodus: The Dust Bowl Migration and Okie Culture in California*. New York: Oxford University Press, 1989.

Grossman, James R. *Land of Hope: Chicago, Black Southerners and the Great Migration*. Chicago: University of Chicago Press, 1989.

Harwood, Elgin, S. *Work and Community among Urban Newcomers: A Study of the Social and Economic Adaptation of Southern Migrants in Chicago*. (Unpublished Ph.D. diss. University of Chicago, 1966).

Herron, Jerry. Afterculture: *Detroit and the Humiliation of History*. Detroit: Wayne State University Press, 1995.

Highest, Phillip and Hoes Hiss, eds. *Local Community Fact Book, 1949*. Chicago: University of Chicago. 1953.

Hoyt, Homer. *One Hundred Years of Land Values in Chicago*. Chicago: University of Chicago Press, 1923.

Hundley, John R. "The Mountain Man in Northern Industry." *Mountain Life and Work*. Vol. 31, No. 2 (1955): 33–38.

Hunter, Albert. *Symbolic Communities: The Persistence and Change of Chicago's Local Communities*. Chicago: University of Chicago Press, 1974.

Jameson, Frederic. *Postmodernism, or, the Cultural Logic of Late Capitalism*. Durham: University of North Carolina Press, 1991.

Jones, Jacqueline. *The Dispossessed: America's Underclasses from the Civil War to the Present*. New York: Basic Books, 1993.

Killian, Lewis M. "Southern White Laborers in Chicago's West Side." (Unpublished Ph.D. diss. University of Chicago, 1949).

———. "The Effects of Southern White Workers on Race Relations in Northern Plants." *American Sociological Review*, 17 (1952):327–331

———. "The Adjustment of Southern White Migrants to Northern Urban Norms," *Social Forces*, Vol. 32 No.1 (1953):66–69.

———. *White Southerners*. New York: Random House, 1970.

Kitagawa, Evelyn and Karl E. Taber, Eds. *Local Community Fact Book, 1960*. Chicago: University of Chicago Press, 1963.

Korral, Virginia Sánchez. *From Colonia to Community.* Berkley: University of California Press, 1994.

Lange, Dorthea and Paul Taylor. *An American Exodus: A Record of Human Erosion.* New York: 1939.

Lee, Everett S. "A Theory of Migration," *Demography,* Vol. 3 No. 1(1966):47–57.

Leeds, Morton. "The Process of Cultural Stripping and Reintegration: The Rural Migrant in the City." *Journal of American Folklore,* 183 No. 328 (1970):259–267.

LeMasters, E.E. *Blue-Collar Aristocrats: Life-Styles at a Working Class Tavern.* Madison: University of Wisconsin Press, 1975.

Leybourne, Grace G. "Urban Adjustment of Migrants from the Southern Appalachian Plateaus," *Social Forces,* 2 No. 16 (1937):238–246.

Logan, John R. and Harvey Molotch. *Urban Fortunes: The Political Economy of Place.* Berkley: University of California Press, 1987.

Long, Larry H. "Poverty Status and Receipt of Welfare Among Migrants and Non-migrants in Large Cities," *American Sociological Review* 39, (1974):46–56.

Marciniak, Ed. "Reversing Urban Decline: The Winthrop-Kenmore Corridor in the Edgewater and Uptown Communities of Chicago." (Washington D.C.:National Center for Urban Ethnic Affairs, 1981:26–49.

Mauldin, W. Parker. "Selective Migration From Small Towns." *American Sociological Review* 5, No. 5 (1940):748–768.

Mell, Mildred. "Poor Whites of the South." *Social Forces* 17, No.1 (1938):153–167.

Merton, Don Edward. "Up Here Down Home: Appalachian Migrants in Northtown," (Unpublished diss. University of Chicago, 1974).

Montgomery, Bill, 1968. "The Uptown Story." *Mountain Life and Work,* (September, 1968):8–18.

National Council of Jewish Women. "The Unaccepted Baltimoreans: A Report on the White Southern Rural Migrants." (unpublished report by the Baltimore section of the National Council of Jewish Women, May 1961).

Newcomb, Charles and Richard O. Lang, *Census Data for the City of Chicago, 1934,* Chicago: University of Chicago Press, 1935.

Northwestern Elevated Railroad, *Where and How to Go,* Chicago: Northwestern Elevated Railroad, 1908.

O'Brian, Ruth. "Buena Park," in *History of the Uptown Community,* Vivian Palmer, ed. Chicago: Historical Society and the Local Community Research Committee, University of Chicago, 1930.

Obermiller, Phillip J. and William Philliber, eds. *Too Few Tomorrows: Urban Appalachians in the 1980's.* Boone, North Carolina: Appalachian Consortium Press, 1987.

Obermiller, Phillip J. and Michael E. Malony. "Looking for Appalachians in Pittsburgh: Seeking 'Deliverance' and Finding the 'Deer Hunter'" *Pittsburgh History* 73, No. 4 (1990):160–169.

Philliber, William. *Appalachian Migrants in Urban America: Cultural Conflict or*

Ethnic Group Formation? New York: Pregaer, 1981.

Philliber, William and Clyde McCoy, eds. *The Invisible Minority: Urban Appalachians.* Lexington: University of Kentucky Press, 1981.

Powles, William E. "The Southern Appalachian Migrant: Country Boy Turned Blue-Collarite," in Arthur Shostak and William Gomberg *Blue Collar World: Studies of the American Worker.* New Jersey: Prentice-Hall, 1964.

Portes, Alejandro. "Migration and Underdevelopment." *Politics and Society* 8, No. 1 (1978):1–48.

Reckless, Walter C. *Vice in Chicago,* Chicago: University of Chicago Press, 1933.

Roncker, Lieutenant Robert. "The Southern Appalachian Migrant: A Study of His Attitudes, Customs and Environment." (Unpublished report Cincinnati Division of Police, August 1959.)

Sánchez, George J. *Becoming Mexican American: Ethnicity, Culture and Identity in Chicano Los Angeles, 1900–1945.* New York: Oxford University Press, 1993.

Schloss, Bert. "The Uptown Area and the Southern White In-Migrant." (an unpublished report Chicago Commission on Human Relations, 1957).

Scott, Shaunna. *Where There is No Middle Ground: Community and Class Consciousness in Harlan County Kentucky.* (Unpublished Ph.D. diss. University of Kentucky, 1988).

Scwarzweller, Harry and John F. Seggar. "Kinship Involvement: A Factor in Adjustment of Rural Migrants." *Journal of Marriage and the Family* 29 (1967):662–671.

Shapiro, Harry. *Appalachia on Our Mind.* Chapel Hill: University of North Carolina Press, 1978.

Sharp, Laurie M., Gene B. Peterson and Thomas F. Drury. *Southern Newcomers to Northern Cities: Work and Social Adjustment in Cleveland.* New York: Praeger, 1977.

Shryock, Henry S. and Charles Nam. 1965. "Educational Selectivity of Interregional Migration." *Social Forces* 43, No. 3 (1965):299–310.

Stekert, Ellen J. 1970. "Focus of Conflict: Southern Mountain Medical Beliefs in Detroit." *Journal of American Folklore* 183, No. 328 (1970):115–152.

Teaford, Jon C. *The Rough Road to Renaissance: Urban Revitalization in America, 1940–1985,* Baltimore: Johns Hopkins, 1990.

Tuan, Yi Fu. *Space and Place: The Perspective of Experience,* Minneapolis: University of Minnesota Press, 1977.

Votaw, Albert. "The Hillbillies Invade Chicago." *Harper's* (February, 1969):64–67.

Welfare Council of Metropolitan Chicago. "Cultural Patterns of Newcomers: Selected Papers."(Unpublished report Welfare Council of Metropolitan Chicago, 1957).

West Virginia State Government. *Annual Report and Directory of Mines,* 1986.

Whisnant, David E. *Modernizing the Mountaineer* Boone: Appalachian Consortium Press, 1980.